A School Leader's Guide to Implementing the Common Core

This accessible resource addresses the problems, challenges, and issues that general and special education leaders frequently face on a day-to-day basis in implementing the Common Core State Standards in their schools. Grounded in best practices from current literature, this text provides leaders with practical solutions to working with teachers and differentiating instruction for all students—including students with special needs as well as ESL and ELL students. *A School Leader's Guide to Implementing the Common Core* presents a cohesive framework and offers viable options for effective inclusive instruction based on students' varied learning needs.

Special features:

- Includes vignettes and "Research-Based Practical Tips" that offer concrete connections to school contexts and illustrate practical applications.
- Explores current trends in Universal Design for Learning (UDL), Multi-tiered Systems of Support (MTSS), and Response to Intervention (RTI), and how they relate to the Common Core State Standards.
- Guides leaders through the development of effective policies for culturally responsive instruction in the classroom.

Gloria D. Campbell-Whatley is Associate Professor of Special Education at the University of North Carolina at Charlotte, USA.

David M. Dunaway is Associate Professor of Educational Leadership at the University of North Carolina at Charlotte, USA.

Dawson R. Hancock is Professor of Educational Research and Associate Dean for Research and Graduate Studies in the College of Education at the University of North Carolina at Charlotte, USA.

Other Eye On Education Books Available from Routledge
(www.routledge.com/eyeoneducation)

How to Make Data Work: A Guide for Educational Leaders
Jenny Grant Rankin

Mentoring Is a Verb: Strategies for Improving College and Career Readiness
Russ Olwell

What Connected Educators Do Differently
Todd Whitaker, Jeffrey Zoul, and Jimmy Casas

BRAVO Principal! Building Relationships with Actions that Value Others, 2nd Edition
Sandra Harris

Get Organized! Time Management for School Leaders, 2nd Edition
Frank Buck

The Educator's Guide to Writing a Book: Practical Advice for Teachers and Leaders
Cathie E. West

Data, Data Everywhere: Bringing All the Data Together for Continuous School Improvement, 2nd Edition
Victoria Bernhardt

Leading Learning for Digital Natives: Combining Data and Technology in the Classroom
Rebecca J. Blink

The Trust Factor: Strategies for School Leaders
Julie Peterson Combs, Stacey Edmonson, and Sandra Harris

The Assistant Principal's Guide: New Strategies for New Responsibilities
M. Scott Norton

The Principal as Human Resources Leader: A Guide to Exemplary Practices for Personnel Administration
M. Scott Norton

Formative Assessment Leadership: Identify, Plan, Apply, Assess, Refine
Karen L. Sanzo, Steve Myran, and John Caggiano

Easy and Effective Professional Development: The Power of Peer Observation to Improve Teaching
Catherine Beck, Paul D'Elia, and Michael W. Lamond

Job-Embedded Professional Development: Support, Collaboration, and Learning in Schools
Sally J. Zepeda

Leading Schools in an Era of Declining Resources
J. Howard Johnston and Ronald Williamson

Creating Safe Schools: A Guide for School Leaders, Teachers, and Parents
Franklin P. Schargel

A School Leader's Guide to Implementing the Common Core

Inclusive Practices for All Students

Gloria D. Campbell-Whatley
David M. Dunaway
Dawson R. Hancock

NEW YORK AND LONDON

First published 2016
by Routledge
711 Third Avenue, New York, NY 10017

and by Routledge
2 Park Square, Milton Park, Abingdon, Oxon, OX14 4RN

Routledge is an imprint of the Taylor & Francis Group, an informa business

© 2016 Taylor & Francis

The right of Gloria D. Campbell-Whatley, David M. Dunaway, and Dawson R. Hancock to be identified as author of this work has been asserted by them in accordance with sections 77 and 78 of the Copyright, Designs and Patents Act 1988.

All rights reserved. No part of this book may be reprinted or reproduced or utilized in any form or by any electronic, mechanical, or other means, now known or hereafter invented, including photocopying and recording, or in any information storage or retrieval system, without permission in writing from the publishers.

Trademark notice: Product or corporate names may be trademarks or registered trademarks, and are used only for identification and explanation without intent to infringe.

Library of Congress Cataloging-in-Publication Data
Names: Campbell-Whatley, Gloria D., author. | Dunaway, David M., author. | Hancock, Dawson R. author.
Title: A school leader's guide to implementing the common core : inclusive practices for all students / Gloria D. Campbell-Whatley, David M. Dunaway, Dawson Hancock.
Description: New York, NY : Routledge, 2016. | Includes bibliographical references.
Identifiers: LCCN 2015031459 | ISBN 9781315769868 (hardback)
Subjects: LCSH: Common Core State Standards (Education) | Inclusive education—United States.
Classification: LCC LB3060.83 .C365 2016 | DDC 379.1/580973—dc23
LC record available at http://lccn.loc.gov/2015031459

ISBN: 978-1-138-78145-0 (hbk)
ISBN: 978-1-138-78146-7 (pbk)
ISBN: 978-1-315-76986-8 (ebk)

Typeset in Bembo
by Book Now Ltd, London

Printed and bound in the United States of America by Sheridan

Contents

Preface		*vii*
Meet the Authors		*xiii*

1	Understanding the Common Core *Gloria D. Campbell-Whatley and David M. Dunaway*	1
2	Connecting the Dots to Educational Planning *Keonya Booker and Gloria D. Campbell-Whatley*	21
3	Data–Driven Formal and Informal Measures *Chuang Wang, Dawson R. Hancock, and Gloria D. Campbell-Whatley*	37
4	Young Children and Their Families *Vivian I. Correa, Ya-yu Lo, and Dawson R. Hancock*	52
5	English Learners: It's More Than Getting an Interpreter *Diane Rodriguez and Gloria D. Campbell-Whatley*	71
6	Children in Urban Centers *Gloria D. Campbell-Whatley, Keonya Booker, Derrick Robinson, and Bettie Butler*	84
7	Children with Disabilities and Those At Risk *Irene Meier, Nicole Conners, and Gloria D. Campbell-Whatley*	101
8	The Common Core Standards, UDL, RTI: Marriage, Merger, Partnership *Christopher O'Brien, Gloria D. Campbell-Whatley, Ozalle Toms, and Christie L. Felder*	123
9	Differentiating the Common Core Curriculum *Rebecca A. Shore, David M. Dunaway, and Gloria D. Campbell-Whatley*	137

Preface

The basic structure and expectations of public education—the system of public education—are largely unchanged since the first public schools in America were established in the 17th century. America's schools were historically built purposefully to sift and sort according to students' intellectual ability. Those with greater demonstrated ability moved on within schools to advanced classes and from schools to universities and then to professional careers. Those with lesser success in schools were relegated to basic classes and moved on toward blue-collar work, dropping out often before graduation. As late as the mid-1990s, this was not an obstacle to earning a comfortable middle-class income. Industrial America provided honest work and a living wage for blue-collar worker.

Today, those options do not exist for American students; whether intentional or incidental, the sift-and-sort philosophy remains firmly entrenched in the culture of public education. Efforts have been made across the years to improve public education, but few of those efforts suggested a change in the culture of the entire profession. Effective schools and efforts like it emphasized the belief that all children could learn at a high level. Charter schools were created as an effort to change the system-in-place, but they tend to act, look, and perform much like the schools they were to replace. No Child Left Behind (NCLB) established a set of punitive measures if schools did not meet certain goals, but even the sweeping NCLB did not cause a change in the system-in-place.

However, at least as early as 2008 the idea of the development of a set of standards that presented what students should know and be able to do by each grade was proposed by the National Governors Association. Today those standards are known as the Common Core State Standards (CCSS). The work toward this set of expectations proposed for adoption by each state changed the metaphor of the system-in-place from sift-and-sort to a pipeline of success—an inclusive pipeline of equal diameter at both ends.

While this change may sound rather subtle, it is far from it. The metaphor of the pipeline requires the change of a professional culture that has not just existed but thrived with sift-and-sort as a primary behavior. That is what cultures do. The actions of the people in the culture are developed in order to solve a problem they are facing. Over time, those actions become unquestioned truths and the actions become unconscious behaviors. So changing a culture begins with changing beliefs. Not necessarily. Just as actions led to "truths" of the system-in-place, so must actions precede the major change in beliefs necessary to fulfill the vision of learning for all and establishing the new truths of higher expectations for all. In other words, before we believe differently, we must behave differently. When success comes from a change in behavior, a new cultural tenet is established.

The CCSS are the impetus for significant cultural change within the school as an organization. We recognize that culture change within any organization is incredibly difficult and not to be embarked upon lightly.

- It demands that old, unquestioned "truths" of the organization be abandoned for new ways of thinking and—more importantly—of behaving.

- It requires new organizational metaphors, procedures, and methods down to the most basic level.

A School Leader's Guide to Implementing the Common Core is written with inclusive practices at the heart of each chapter. In each chapter, you will find the practical means—frequently with specific examples—needed to assure that the CCSS are fully and faithfully implemented so that every child is included not just philosophically but practically and realistically.

A School Leader's Guide to Implementing the Common Core engages leaders in effective practical applications as they employ critical thinking about problem-solving techniques with teachers. This guide is grounded in best practices from current literature for leaders with applications for staff, teachers, parents, and students. The text is written from a practical perspective targeting building-level and special education leaders. Both special education and general education leaders such as Department of Instruction personnel, professors of special education, and professors of educational leadership have input in the text.

The book offers and solidly defines how the CCSS, Universal Design for Learning (UDL), Response to Intervention (RTI), and Multi-tiered Systems of Support (MTSS) merge. Vignettes within the chapters that apply these principles to elementary, middle, and high school youngsters in various environments provide concrete applications. With the large influx of English language learners (ELLs) in urban settings, the book discusses practical applications to address these environments and engages the reader to be able to apply them to similar circumstances through practical situational analysis.

Leaders desire innovative insight for working with special education issues in a similar context. Present administrative texts offer little to the aspiring school leader in this regard. Most current texts related to school leaders and special education have the "law" flavor and quote rules and regulations outside of a situational context, whereas this text uses vignettes to apply the concepts of problem solving. Also, the guide allows for a variety of evidence-based strategies for effective special and general education leadership practices.

Chapter 1 introduces the reader to the framework of the CCSS as a United States (U.S.) education initiative that seeks to bring diverse state curricula into alignment by following the principles of standards-based education reform. The CCSS and their key components as they relate to general education relative to the goals, rigor, criteria, assessment, and evidence-based instruction are discussed.

General and special education has a number of shared initiatives. Chapter 2 guides building-level and special education leaders in knowledge related to devising a cohesive and collaborative Common Core curriculum for general and special education teachers. Leaders are directed through the legalities of the Individuals with Disabilities Education Act (IDEA) and the Elementary and Secondary Education Act and ways they combine to produce appropriate instruction and assessment for all children.

Chapter 3 provides descriptions of the two consortia, Partnership for Assessment of Readiness for College and Career (PARCC) and the Smarter Balanced Assessment Consortium (SBAC), and various formative classroom-based assessments that can be used in conjunction with them. Assessment practices are connected to instruction in this chapter and finally a classroom walk-through tool is provided for school leaders to assess teachers' implementation of the standards and measures.

The CCSS have been devised for young children, and states need alternate core curriculum materials to teach general education and students with disabilities in kindergarten through third grade using evidence-based interventions and procedures. Seldom do the needs of children with disabilities divide neatly along program lines. Instead, children and their families navigate a large, complex, and fragmented array of programs with inconsistent eligibility standards, application procedures, and program goals. *Meeting the needs of children with disabilities* causes leaders to become advocates and build a vision for an integrated system centered on children and families. Chapter 4 describes the Common Core curriculum for young children and their families.

There are a large number of students in America's classrooms today, causing a demand for additional programs and services. Unfortunately, there are many critical issues that relate to ELLs that revolve around standards instruction and assessment as related to culture. There is a need to integrate cultural literature into disciplines and content as well as language differences and nuances, especially in the core curriculum and standards-based instruction. Sometimes ELL instruction is considered a separate entity from standard-based instruction but should be an infused entity; in fact, they are intertwined. Assessment of ELLs is another concern because these students are excluded from test and sometimes are expected to participate in assessments that make inaccurate assumptions about language proficiency as well as content knowledge. In many classes, content is not connected to the students' background, creating a large gap between knowledge and experience. Because of these issues and the additional label for special services, the effectiveness of instruction is not realized. Chapter 5 focuses on these issues as it relates to school-based and special education leaders and ELLs.

As more students from diverse ethnic, cultural, and social backgrounds enter public schools, leaders must provide an enriching learning environment that encourages academic equality and achievement. Such a learning environment would acknowledge the importance of integrating cultural and personal experiences that students bring with them to the classroom structure. The promise of effective infusion of culturally responsive instruction within the classroom provides students with greater chances for academic success; however, the challenge is making it happen. Chapter 6 focuses on school-based and special education leaders and the development of academic success in an urban climate.

Students with disabilities are going to be challenged to excel within the general curriculum and be prepared for success in their post-school lives; this includes college and/or careers. According to the Individuals with Disabilities Education Act (IDEA), each student with a disability has Individualized Education Plan (IEP), and educational planning is determined on an individual basis. The standards are rigorous, yet students with disabilities may not be able to match that rigor. Chapter 7 outlines the infusion of the CCSS into the educational plans of the students with disabilities, students under 504, and students at risk and the services and accommodations to support them.

An increased accountability in schools in recent years has presented enormous challenges to public schools seeking to teach rigorous curricula to a population of students with diverse backgrounds and abilities. Chapter 8 discusses the current trends toward RTI, MTSS, and UDL and other methods that promote inclusion for all students and how they relate to CCSS.

Differentiated instruction is teaching students according to their strengths and creating learning opportunities using varied instruction, rather than a standardized approach. Because each learner comes to school with a different set of learning needs, students are placed at the center of instruction and learning. Chapter 9 explains varied instruction and the Common Core curriculum from an administrative aspect and how varied instructional methods linked to assessment are discussed as related to core instruction and content, process, and product according to the student's way of learning.

For the contributors to *A School Leader's Guide to Implementing the Common Core*, this has been a labor of love among a diverse group of professionals who truly believe that *all means all*. Nonetheless, it has been a laborious undertaking to challenge the cultural underpinnings of a 400-year-old system with practical and realistic strategies designed to successfully implement the CCSS at each school level. With *A School Leader's Guide to Implementing the Common Core*, we provide a set of hands-on practices for beginning and sustaining the cultural changes necessary to authentically implement the CCSS at the school level.

We trust that you as a school or special education leader or an aspiring school leader—whatever that phrase means to you—will put to the test the tactics and strategies found within these pages. And we hope that you will let us know of your successes so that we can build this new culture of inclusiveness together.

Finally, we offer our genuine thanks and gratitude to all the authors who provided information to this book. Their collective wisdom demonstrates the power of synergy. This work is not a collection of independent contributions, but rather a gathering of individuals committed to a common belief in the possible. They are a "failure is not an option" kind of group and that defining characteristic has produced a work that surpasses a mere collection of work by like-minded people working individually. Collectively, they added immensely to the knowledge and expertise that is reflected in this book.

These authors include our faculty colleagues and graduate students at the University of North Carolina at Charlotte: Dr. Vivian Correa, Dr. Rebecca Shore, Dr. Chris O'Brien, Dr. Ya-yu Lo, Dr. Chuang Wang, Dr. Bettie Butler, and Derrick Robinson.

Other authors include Dr. Diane Rodriguez of Fordham University; Dr. Irene Meier, Director, Office of Special Education Instruction, Fairfax County Public Schools; Nicole Conners, Office of Special Education Instruction, Fairfax County Public Schools; Dr. Ozalle M. Toms, University of Wisconsin at Whitewater; Dr. Keonya Booker, College of Charleston; and Christie Felder, a student at Winthrop University. We thank Xinyi Zhang, a graduate of the University of North Carolina at Charlotte for her superb use of APA.

Meet the Authors

Gloria D. Campbell-Whatley is an Associate Professor in the Department of Special Education and Child Development at the University of North Carolina at Charlotte. She serves as a teacher of graduate students there and has been the graduate coordinator. She received her doctorate of education at the University of Alabama at Tuscaloosa. She has delivered numerous national and international presentations, workshops, and strands. Her specialty is infusing diversity into higher education and K–12 curriculum, and she also offers solutions for behavior problems, response to intervention, and social skills training in public schools. Dr. Campbell-Whatley has written several articles related to multicultural education and published two books on behavior and an administrative textbook. Her research focuses on diversity, social skills and behavior, and administration in special education. She has served as a program specialist for Special Education Programs in Birmingham, Alabama. She has also been on the Council for Exceptional Children national and international boards and served as Originator of the Special Education Department at Indiana University-Purdue University, Fort Wayne.

David M. Dunaway is an Associate Professor and Director of Doctoral Programs for the Department of Educational Leadership at the University of North Carolina at Charlotte. He is a frequently published writer and presenter on school organization, leadership, and school improvement. In 2012, Dr. Dunaway received the 2011–12 Annual Faculty Service Award for Sustained Service to Public Schools from the University of North Carolina at Charlotte's College of Education. Previously Dr. Dunaway served as an Assistant Professor at the University of Louisville and as an Adjunct Professor at Auburn University and the University of Southern Indiana. With 35 years in public education at the K–12 level, he has served as a District Superintendent in Gibson County, Indiana, and as Deputy Superintendent for Instruction in the Owensboro Public Schools in Owensboro, Kentucky. In Alabama Dr. Dunaway taught at the middle and high school levels, served as Assistant Principal of a large urban high school, and as a small town High School Principal for a dozen years. As a Principal in

Alabama, Dr. Dunaway served as President of the Alabama High School Principals Association and was selected as Alabama Principal of the Year in 1991. During that same year, he was selected by the National Association of Secondary School Principals as a member of the U.S. delegation to establish a principal exchange program with the Soviet Union. Dr. Dunaway received his Bachelor's Degree from Auburn University in 1969, his MA from the University of South Alabama in 1976, and his ED.D from Auburn University in 1985. As a parent of a disabled child, much of Dr. Dunaway's passion for and knowledge of learning came from his simultaneous roles as parent and school leader.

Dawson R. Hancock currently serves as a Professor of Educational Research and the Associate Dean for Research and Graduate Studies in the University of North Carolina at Charlotte's College of Education. His research interests include assessment and evaluation, curriculum design, student and faculty motivation, and leadership theory and application. His most recent works investigate factors which influence the motivation of teachers to become school leaders. He has published articles in the *International Journal of Educational Research, Journal of Educational Research, Journal of Educational Research and Policy Studies, Educational Technology Research and Development, Journal of Research on Childhood Education, Assessment in Education: Principles, Policy, and Practice, NASSP Bulletin, College Teaching, The Educational Forum, Teacher Education and Practice,* and *Journal of General Education.* He has presented papers at the annual meetings of several international professional organizations, including the European Educational Research Association and the American Educational Research Association. His accomplishments include receipt of the North Carolina Association for Research in Education's Distinguished Paper Award. He has served as Vice President for Research and Measurement of the American Association for Research in Education. In his 19 years of service at the University of North Carolina at Charlotte, he has engaged in extensive research, written numerous journal articles, book chapters, and books, and taught graduate courses in educational research methods, assessment and evaluation methods, program evaluation methods, survey research methods, qualitative research methods, and advanced statistics. Dr. Hancock also has extensive experience working in the public schools of North Carolina, primarily as an evaluator of programs designed to enhance student learning and the preparation and retention of high-quality teachers and administrators.

CHAPTER

Understanding the Common Core

Gloria D. Campbell-Whatley and David M. Dunaway

Mrs. Strict has a problem with the way Mrs. Adapt is teaching the Common Core State Standards to the students in mathematics. The students with learning disabilities are under the Individuals with Disabilities Act (IDEA), and they are supposed to have instruction according to the Individual Education Plan (IEP). Do they really expect me to believe that these students with learning disabilities (LD) are college-bound? Mrs. Strategies, the learning disabilities teacher, wants to come in and perform team teaching with me, but I am unsure of her knowledge. Then there are the Tier 2 students who are at risk. They are expecting me to make accommodations. I have been teaching for 25 years, and I am retiring next year and plan on teaching the way I have always taught. After all, we should be readying the smarter students for college. Isn't that the purpose of the standards? Principal Rules is going to have to settle this difficulty. What is he to do?

Introduction

The Common Core State Standards (CCSS) is a U.S. education initiative that seeks to bring diverse state curricula into alignment by following the principles of standards-based education reform. The goal of the standards is to ensure that students are college- and career-ready at the end of high school. The standards are research- and evidence-based, aligned with college expectations, rigorous, and internationally synonymous for a global society. This chapter will introduce the CCSS and their key components relative to the goals, rigor, criteria, assessment, and evidence-based instruction while addressing the inclusive factor of students with disabilities, at-risk students, young populations, and urban students.

The CCSS connect what is expected of students at each grade level, allowing school-based and special education leaders to properly plan to equip teachers to establish appropriate benchmarks. The standards focus on core concepts starting in the early grades, giving students the opportunity to master them. As these standards are applied across states, new challenges arise as school-based leaders identify special education as a major topic of concern. Students with disabilities are noted in the standards and there is the expectation for them to function within the general curriculum, yet leaders wrestle with the CCSS and how students with special needs will fare in the curriculum (Scruggs, Brigham, & Mastropieri, 2013). It is important that evidenced-based techniques that have a positive effect on students be used as solutions. Because of the many existing principles and evidence-based practices already in effect such as inclusion, Response to Intervention (RTI), Universal Design for Learning (UDL), and other shared concepts, school-based leaders must effectively solve problems and appropriately apply and integrate these concepts (Gamm et al., 2012; Haager, 2013). School-based and special education leaders must now merge the CCSS into these standing strategies and methodologies.

The vignette in the opening of the chapter demonstrates that school and special education leaders may have to provide additional guidance for teachers to assist students, especially those with disabilities, at risk, or in various settings such as rural or urban environments. Not only will teachers be faced with learning and successfully implementing a new set of expectations in their classrooms, but they will need to be aware of the learning needs of culturally and linguistically diverse students. Because of the large influx of immigrants, school-based leaders have to make plans for English language learners (ELLs), which require unique decisions as they relate to the U.S. school systems. These students will be held to the same high standards and rigorous grade-level expectations in the areas of speaking, listening, reading, and writing. Many of these initiatives are implemented in the general education setting; therefore, special education leaders must work collaboratively to assure effective application. Both general and special education leaders must work with specialized clientele and coordinate these aspects of the entire spectrum of responsibilities in the school and need resources to perceive how these concepts link together and operate in unison.

CCSS: An Overview

The standards were created to ensure that all students graduate from high school with the skills and knowledge necessary to succeed in college, career, and life. The criteria were developed by incorporating standards from states in America and foreign countries. Specifically, they are research- and evidence-based and used by other top-performing countries in order to prepare all students for success in our global economy and society (Understanding the Common Core Standards, 2014).

The goal is to produce high-quality academic standards in mathematics, English language arts (E/LA)/literacy, science, and technology while outlining learning goals as to what a student should know and demonstrate at the end of each grade. They define what all students are expected to know and be able to do, not how teachers should teach. In other words, the standards focus on what is most essential, but interventions and strategies are left to the discretion of teachers and curriculum developers. There are standards for content area literacy, but supports for readiness are not fully described for ELLs and for students with special needs.

Almost all states have adopted the CCSS, even with reservations from parents, political figures, and school personnel (Understanding the Common Core Standards, 2014). The standards, launched in 2009, were developed by a group of non-profit and bipartisan organizations rather than federal dollars. These organizations' main interest was to promote higher academic standards (i.e., College Board, ACT). Originally, the standards addressed only E/LA in 2011; however, Achieve Inc., in conjunction with other educational entities (i.e., National Research Council, The National Science Teachers Association, etc.), included science and engineering. The U.S. Department of Education was not involved in developing the standards, but has supported their adoption by providing Race-to-the-Top funding and the development and field-testing of assessments (Understanding the Common Core Standards, 2014). Already, it has been estimated that 85 percent of the mathematics and E/LA content are taught to elementary, middle, and high schools, thereby leaving only 15 percent autonomy for state education and local education agencies (LEAs) (Heitin, 2014).

E/LA and Math Standards

The standards offer guidelines for E/LA and literacy in history/social studies, science, and technical subjects. These are intertwined because students learn to apply language arts skills in the content areas. Therefore, the standards are designed to promote the literacy skills necessary for college and career readiness in multiple and varied disciplines and content areas. In other words, the literacy standards expect teachers to use content areas to help students master reading, writing, speaking, listening, and language through integration of literacy skills across content areas. States determine how to suffuse these standards into their existing standards.

Literacy

The skills and knowledge captured in the E/LA and literacy standards are designed to prepare students for life outside the classroom. Since the standards are designed to prepare students for everyday life, critical thinking skills are heavily used and subscribe to the definition that a truly literate person can incorporate these skills.

Within the standards are design considerations that include vertically aligned expectations with mastery of each grade level to succeed at the next level. The

CCSS define college readiness as the ability to work independently, understand complex information across a wide range of literary and technical sources, and develop the voice to express key points and ideas. The standards emphasize that students should learn to read with purpose, listen rather than just hear, and share their understanding of acquired knowledge through writing and speech.

CCSS require students to communicate according to the uniqueness of the audience, the task, the purpose, and the nature of the content discipline. The goal is to become selective readers and listeners and be able to grasp a writer or speaker's purpose while evaluating the foundations and assumptions presented. Technology including various forms of media is used to communicate meaning and points of view.

The E/LA standards are taught across subjects. Specifically, reading and writing standards are defined for several subjects such as English, history, social studies, science, and technical subjects (Understanding the Common Core Standards, 2014). Reading, writing, discourse, and strategies will depend on the discipline. Instruction will shift from direct instruction and memorization to an integrated complexity of skills to understand multifaceted ideas.

History and Social Studies

Since subjects are infused across the curriculum, the emphasis is on reading, writing, speaking, and listening. Students will need to synthesize, report, reflect, persuade, and use a plethora of academic language. These standards will require skills in investigation and an elaborate dependence on time.

Science and Technical Subjects

Science skills include the identification and examination of problems and specific types of data. Technology will be the forefront as we move instructional devices toward e-reading, audiobooks, and other digital formats of accessing information online. In the 21st century, technology literacy is essential. Students will need to find and evaluate information.

Mathematics

The standards stress conceptual understanding of the laws of arithmetic. Students will have to not only explain their skills but be able to defend their thinking. The math standards are rigorous and emphasize fluency, rigor, speed, and intensity.

The Five Key Components of the Common Core

There are five key components of the CCSS: (a) reading, (b) writing, (c) speaking and listening, (d) language, and (e) mathematics. These are further divided into sub-areas. Although the skills are the same, they scaffold increasingly higher according to grade. A sample chart is provided.

Table 1.1 Elementary, Middle, and High School Grades: Understanding the Flow

Standard	*Subskills*	*Examples of Skill Progression*
Reading		
Literature	Key ideas and details: *Summarize, identify plots, and analyze a story*	**Elementary:** "Who, what, when, how" … the basics of a story develop a sense of character plot and setting **Middle school:** Describe the plot but provide insights on the character, their thoughts, and feelings **High school:** Identify the central theme and be able to analyze the text
	Craft and structure: *The beauty and structure of the language*	**Elementary:** Develop a point of view and determine how words affect meaning (i.e., songs, poems) **Middle school:** Determine word and literary choices and figurative language **High school:** Investigate structure, tone and style of writing
	Integration of knowledge and ideas: *Critical thinking*	**Elementary:** Determining material they like and do not like and collecting experiences through the lives of characters **Middle school:** Comparing and contrasting how different texts may emphasize the same concepts **High school:** Analyze how visual effects and multimedia can add flavor to a text
	Range of reading level and text complexity: *Varied literature (i.e., myth, drama, poetry)*	**Elementary:** Decode, comprehend, read smoothly, and think while reading with prompting and support **Middle school:** Comprehend literature with scaffolding as needed **High school:** Comprehend literature, including stories, dramas, and poems
Informational text	Key ideas and details: *Social studies, science texts, and other disciplines*	**Elementary:** Provide details and the main idea **Middle school:** Extract the central theme, analyzing and using supporting facts **High school:** Use facts and evidence to support arguments
	Craft and structure: *Examining the tone and vocabulary of texts*	**Elementary:** Identify book covers, table of contents, glossaries, menus, icons **Middle school:** Compare and contrast different structures (i.e., cause/effect, problem solution) **High school:** Analyze the structure of paragraphs, refine key concepts, and identify arguments and viewpoints

(Continued)

Table 1.1 (Continued)

Standard	Subskills	Examples of Skill Progression
	Integration of knowledge and ideas: *New information, unfamiliar subjects, new topics*	**Elementary:** Infer details and contexts from images and visuals and oral presentations **Middle school:** Analyze how visuals alter presentation **High school:** Communicate an idea by determining the advantages and disadvantages of using illustrations, print, audio
	Range of reading and text complexity: *Various genres*	**Elementary:** Read text from a broad range of cultures and period, including poetry, drama, stories (i.e., folktales, legends, fables), literary nonfiction, historical, scientific, and technical texts (i.e., charts, maps, digital sources) **Middle school:** Identify subgenres of exposition, argument, functional text in the form of personal essays, speeches, journalism, and historical, scientific, and technical sources **High school:** Identify subgenres of myths, science fiction, allegories, parodies, satire, and graphic novels, sonnets, odes, epics, essays, speeches, opinion pieces and essays
Foundation skills	Print concepts: *Directionality of text* Phonological awareness: *The sounds of language* Phonics and word recognition: *Strategies to decode words* Fluency: *Reading for accuracy, purpose, and understanding*	**Elementary:** Examine and understand the written word **Elementary:** Become aware of the sound of words **Elementary:** Perform word analysis strategies to decode multisyllabic words in and out of context **Elementary:** Read with sufficient accuracy and fluency to support comprehension, word recognition and understanding, and rereading
Writing Types of purposes of text	Argument and opinion: *To persuade and educate and audience*	**Elementary:** Use pictures and opening and concluding sentences to persuade and provide a clear statement of opinion **Middle school:** Strengthen the structure of the argument by collecting evidence logically **High school:** Outline opinions of others and distinguish their points of view through discourse
	Information and explanatory: *Communicating clearly to educate an audience*	**Elementary:** Use a combination of words and pictures to introduce a topic **Middle school:** Use concrete details, domain-specific details, and technical terms about their topic **High school:** Organize written pieces, categorizing information, using formatting, visuals, headings, charts, and graphs to clarify concepts for the audience and using a formal style

	Narrative and storytelling: *Writing about real or imagined stories*	**Elementary:** Determine characters, thoughts, emotions, and reactions to the main event
		Middle school: Use narrative techniques, using dialogue to recount a story and capture characters' reactions to viewpoints
		High school: Use various narrative techniques while establishing a clear context and point of view
Production and distribution of writing		**Elementary:** Use development and organization skills appropriate to task and technology to produce and publish writing in collaboration with others in a purposeful manner
		Middle school: Produce clear and coherent writing whose development, organization, and style are appropriate and to publish writing using the internet
		High school: Develop and strengthen writing by planning, revising, editing, rewriting, or trying a new approach and jointly producing and publishing with others
Research to build present knowledge		**Elementary:** Participate in shared research and writing projects, recall information from experiences, or gather information from provided sources to answer a question.
		Middle school: Perform short research projects to answer a question, drawing on several sources and evidence
		High school: Perform sustained research projects to solve a problem synthesizing multiple sources
Range of writing		**Elementary:** Appreciate that a key purpose of writing is to communicate clearly to an external audience the content of their writing to accomplish a particular task and purpose
		Middle school: Offer and support opinions, demonstrate an understanding of the subjects that are studied, and convey real and imagined experiences
		High school: Build knowledge on a subject through research projects, respond in writing, and produce pieces
Listening and speaking Comprehension and collaboration		**Elementary:** Understand text read aloud or information presented orally or through other media
		Middle school: Engage in collaborative discussions on various issues, expressing ideas, probe and reflect on ideas
		High school: Express ideas clearly and persuasively using researched material, evidence, rhetoric, assessing the stance, premises, word choice, points of emphasis, and tone

(Continued)

Table 1.1 (Continued)

Standard	Subskills	Examples of Skill Progression
Vocabulary acquisition and use		**Elementary:** Describe people, places, and things that are familiar and progress to recounting a story, experience, or feeling **Middle school:** Adapt tone and language for varied settings and examine complex subjects including facts and key points **High school:** Becoming confident in front of an audience with visual and interactive components
Language Conventions of Standard English		**Elementary:** Correct use of punctuation, spelling, and complex tenses **Middle school:** Using the proper case, dissecting pronouns **High school:** Verbs in the active and passive voice and indicate moods (i.e., interrogative, subjunctive)
Knowledge of language		**Elementary:** Using formal and informal language and refining sentences **Middle school:** Refine sentences and dialects so that they are more meaningful **High school:** Writing sentences that manipulate verbs to express feelings and actions
Vocabulary acquisition and use		**Elementary:** Identify new meanings for words, sort words by category, find opposites, act out words for a similar action **Middle school:** Examine affixes from various languages, using reference material, digital resources and finding meanings for various phrases **High school:** Use figurative language, irony, and distinguishing the association of words with the similar definitions
Mathematics Mathematical content		**Elementary:** Use concrete objects or pictures to help conceptualize and solve a problem **Middle school:** Analyze and make conjectures about the form and meaning of a solution pathway and monitor and evaluate their progress and change course if necessary **High school:** Transform algebraic expressions, use a graphing calculator, explain correspondences between equations, tables, and graphs

Standards for mathematical practice	Reason abstractly and quantitatively: *Make sense of quantities and their relationships in problem situations*	**Elementary:** Understand the basics such as addition, subtraction, whole number, place value, linear measurement, geometric shapes, fractions, division integrating decimal fractions, decimals, and volume
		Middle school: Understand ratio and rate, rational negative numbers, writing, interpreting equations, and statistical thinking
		High school: Understand bivariate data with linear equations, quantitative relationships, analyzing dimensional space and figures, and applying the Pythagorean theorem
	Construct viable arguments and critique the reasoning of others: *State assumptions, definitions, and previously established results in constructing arguments*	**Elementary:** Construct arguments using concrete referents such as objects, drawings, diagrams, and actions.
		Middle school: Generalize and determine domains to which an argument applies
		High school: Use stated assumptions, definitions, and previously established results in constructing arguments, making conjectures, and analyzing situations
	Model with mathematics: *Apply the mathematics to solve problems in everyday life, society, and the workplace*	**Elementary:** Write an addition equation to describe a situation
		Middle school: Apply proportional reasoning to analyze a problem in real life
		High school: Solving a design problem or apply what is known by making an assumption
	Use appropriate tools strategically: *Consider tools when solving a mathematical problem*	**Elementary:** Use of tools such as pencil and paper, concrete models, a ruler, protractor, or calculator
		Middle and high school: Analyze graphs of functions and solutions generated using a graphing calculator and detect possible errors by strategic estimation and other mathematical knowledge
	Attend to precision: *Use clear definitions in discussion with others and in their own reasoning*	**Elementary:** Give carefully formulated explanations, state the meaning of the symbols they choose, such as using the equal sign
		Middle and high school: Examine claims and make explicit use of definitions
	Look for and make use of structure: *Look closely to discern a pattern or structure*	**Elementary:** Understand the associative property
		Middle school: Understand an auxiliary line for solving problems
		High school: Understand complicated patterns such as some algebraic expressions
	Look for and express regularity in repeated reasoning: *Calculations are repeated, and look both for general methods and shortcuts*	**Elementary:** Notice repeated calculations
		Middle school: Notice the abstract equation
		High school: Evaluate the reasonableness of results

What about the Curriculum?

Leaders can no longer accept "covering" the curriculum and moving forward without student mastery as an acceptable professional practice. Teachers and school leaders are going to need ongoing professional development to be able to understand, apply, analyze, and evaluate agreed-upon rubrics as evidence of students' mastery of standards. Teachers as well as school leaders need to be trained in the use of collaboration techniques if they are to have important roles in transforming the curriculum, instruction, and learning. The currently accepted understanding of the purpose and structure of school schedules, differentiation of instruction, coteaching, remediation, and instructional planning must be redesigned.

What about students with disabilities? The CCSS say little about students with severe and mild disabilities or those at risk. For students with severe disabilities, a common set of standards will not verify clear benchmarks, yet, students with severe disabilities should have the opportunity to learn these standards (Courtade, Spooner, Browder, & Jimenez, 2012), but the curriculum may not be right for all students. There is mention of braille and screen-reader technology, but as in many other education-wide initiatives, special education is an afterthought (Haager, 2013).

There are other groups that CCSS slightly mentions—ELL populations. In recent years there has been an increase of school-aged ELL students across the nation. Research has shown that urban students may need different school structures. In fact, at successful schools, 75 percent of ELL students show sustained positive results (Manley & Hawkins, 2013). Therefore, teachers must learn alternate and varied approaches and strategies such as culturally relevant pedagogy, UDL, and other methods that involve real-world applications. The teacher in the vignette will need to develop these skills with the help of local leaders and administrators. Dalley (2012) studied teachers in high-achieving urban and diverse settings and found that students of teachers who were willing to change and adapt their methods of teaching were more likely to reach mastery. Leaders will need to do the following:

- Design collaborative learning environments.
- Monitor, collect, and communicate about data related to benchmarks and assessment.
- Secure adequate training and resources for teachers and parents.
- Establish budget priorities necessary to reach the goals.
- Collaborate with special education leaders to assure resources for students with disabilities and for those academically at risk.
- Design processes for aligning the curriculum, instruction, and assessment to the classroom level and assure that the learning expectations are rigorous, precise, exact, accurate, and thorough as well as culturally sensitive.

- Develop operating principles that guide the faculty through new routines, new culture, and new rules.
- Involve all certified staff members in mapping and aligning the curriculum.
- Provide time within the schedule for staff to collaborate on implementing aligned curriculum and instruction.
- Teach, require, and review lesson plans to assure that Bloom's taxonomy is used as the basis for instruction and assessment.
- Teach all staff members how to lead through collaboration, monitor and improve student learning, and assess the implementation of best collaborative processes such as the use of learning communities.
- Facilitate faculty's understanding and application of the standards to locally developed curriculum and assessments and in alignment with the needs of the students.

Elementary

Elementary school leaders must rethink the assignment of teachers in order to match teacher skills and grade-level expectations. For example, teachers with strong literacy and math skills may serve as integrative specialists who can create and demonstrate lessons for colleagues. Elementary leaders must become experts in and advocates for strategies for urban children, immigrants, and children with special needs.

Middle School

Middle school leaders embrace their unique role as communication catalyst between elementary and high schools. They must create and routinely use communication channels between previous learning in elementary school and future learning in high school. They must be knowledgeable of both elementary and high school standards and assure instructional alignment such that teachers are building upon the students' previous learning and readying students for the increasingly complex future task.

High School

Leaders must first recognize the small amount of time they have to meet the expectations of college and career readiness. Therefore, a palpable sense of urgency is suggested as a common trait of all staff members. Leaders will need to creatively utilize time as a critical resource and protect the academic day (Education Commission of the States, 1994/2005).

Leaders intuitively understand the requirement of changing from the system in place and creating new processes, new ways of thinking, and new ways of working together. Collaboration is, again, the starting place and school leaders are its expert facilitators.

We Stand United: Why Are the Common Core Standards Needed?

The standards are designed to be robust and relevant to the real world, reflecting the knowledge and skills that our young people need for success in college and careers. With American students fully prepared for the future, our communities will be best positioned to compete successfully in the global economy. The CCSS provide a *national framework* of student and teacher expectation—a change in the landscape of education that has been in place since the creation of the United States (Manley & Hawkins, 2013).

The CCSS are important for a number of obvious reasons. First, as the United States has been less successful than other countries in student achievement, the role of a national curriculum has been noted as a reason why other countries perform higher (Manley & Hawkins, 2013). Second, careers are changing in the United States and the upcoming workforce will require that new skills be taught in schools. Third, the CCSS will align participating states to the same expectations. Fourth, collaboration among teachers and schools will increase as all will be operating on the same set of standards. Students will not need to experience a dramatic change in curriculum as they move from one state to another. Fifth, research, literacy, and media skills are interlaced throughout the standards; therefore, students will increase and expand their thinking, writing, and teaching skills. Dunkle (2012) believes that teachers will become architects of information because it gives them increased flexibility in what, how, and when to teach. The standards act more as a guide rather than a checklist, thereby creating the potential for teachers to have students engaged in the curriculum (Dana, Burns, & Wolkenhauer, 2013). However, this vision is not shared by everyone.

Opposition

A number of groups oppose the standards and believe they will cause more testing accountability (Understanding the Common Core Standards, 2014). The Gallup Poll of the Superintendent's Panel (2013) shows that less than a quarter (21 percent) of the states that have agreed to implement the standards believe that the CCSS will give the United States a competitive edge. Over a third of public school parents (35 percent) have a positive impression of the CCSS; therefore, consensus is far from assured.

Educational leaders have a number of concerns about CCSS. Less than a half of superintendents (44 percent) agree that teachers in their district are well prepared to teach the CCSS. Only a half of superintendents (50 percent) agree that the teachers in their district are prepared to support students with disabilities and ESL students.

According to some scholars, the CCSS are so revolutionary that it will radically change the present K–12 system (Ayres, 2012). Others question the legitimacy of the CCSS, declaring that the standards are nothing but a business venture by the College Board in response to a diminishing number of students taking the SAT (Understanding the Common Core Standards, 2014).

Education at the state level has been traditionally a function of local boards of education (LEAs) whose powers are derived directly from the state legislatures, except for Hawaii which has only a state system. Local boards, through their policies and administrative procedures, have authorized very broad and diverse expectations for their schools. At the local level (the district and increasingly the school), education can be encapsulated in the double entendre of "everyday democracy." Citizens most commonly encounter their government in the form of school board members, district and school personnel. It is therefore the level where parents, as citizens, influence and affect change that they can directly observe. Recently the CCSS has tested the practical authority of local boards in speed, scope, and impact on the educational landscape. Moving forward in light of the well-intended and ill-intended—the positive and negative, the meaningful and meaningless—discussion is essential if school leaders are to successfully navigate and lead in the era of the CCSS.

Ujifusa (2014) mentions several other difficulties with adopting and implementing CCSS. He states that there is no real way to measure the success of the standards. Right now, we have the state's activities to implement, but numerous factors are considered such as resources, professional development, and support to implement the standards. Different states have different levels of resources and are making efforts to collaborate with regional entities and districts to make the enormous shifts in assessments, content, and alignment to curricular. It is difficult to ascertain if the teachers who have the resources are using them properly.

With difficulties such as these, whether real or perceived, leadership must assert itself in myriad behaviors, forms, and strategies if CCSS is to succeed. Therefore, leaders in the era of the CCSS must create and sustain leadership focused on leading all children, all teachers, all families, and all communities with a vision for social justice unlike any seen heretofore. When asked by an audience member, "What does learning for all really mean?," Dr. Larry Lezotte, a founder of the Effective Schools Process, said fondly, usually with a wry smile, "All means all, and that is all that all means." In the era of leadership in the Common Core, no child is hidden—purposefully or unconsciously. With the CCSS, schools have the simple but profound mission of graduating students who are ready to go to work and/or continue with their education. Not some children but all!

School Environmental Challenges and Solutions: Smoothing Rough Places

"There is nothing more difficult to take in hand, more perilous to conduct, or more uncertain in its success, than to take the lead in the introduction of a new order of things," wrote Niccolo Machiavelli in *The Prince* (1513). Understanding the Common Core Standards (2014) suggests several challenges with the implementation of CCSS. First, assessment and accountability measures need field-testing. Second, modifications and accommodations should be designed for students with disabilities (Haager, 2013). Third, teaching and learning strategies need to be developed that utilize technologies. Fourth, professional development, a consistently underperforming area of the profession, must be redesigned to align curriculum and instruction to the classroom level. With an estimate of $27.00 more per student to fund these changes in the curriculum, professional development must be a budget priority at the state, district, and school levels (Heitin, 2014).

School-Based Leaders

School leaders will likely reflect even more often on the perilous nature of school cultural change in the era of the Common Core. Leaders in the area of special education are just as likely to look upon the changing nature of their roles with trepidation in this cultural shift. Too often, both school and leaders have "led" with a legalistic policy and process orientation toward special education. Visionary leadership in the era of the Common Core will place management of policies secondary to leading for learning and mastery. This is most critical for the at-risk populations for whom the school is often the only source of learning. There are no insurmountable barriers. Not for the poor. Not for the immigrant.

Leadership in the era of the CCSS must be collaborative at its very core and in its application. The road ahead is simply too rough and the elevation too steep for any one individual to successfully navigate his or her organization to successful implementation. School boards will need to assure that they supply appropriate resources. The changes will need to be communicated to parents, and school boards must serve as advocates to guarantee that the changes that are implemented are supported at the state capital, the district office, and in individual classrooms (Understanding the Common Core Standards, 2014).

In general, school leadership and teaching to date has been an inexact art that too often lacks the precision and reliability of other professions' accepted best practices. The level of learning required of school personnel is large. Educators must learn, embrace, and use new methods consistent with the values of education that is socially just and with high expectations for all students.

No longer can schools purposefully or insidiously practice the "my poor babies syndrome" (Dunaway, 2009) where teachers lower expectations on students in order to protect them from failure. In the era of the CCSS, no longer can poor teaching be excused because of poverty, race, or place of birth, or disability of the students being served. No longer can pseudo-leadership be the accepted norm where the "my poor babies syndrome" flourishes.

Special Education Leaders

There is something unrealistic about measuring students with disabilities with the same standards as those without disabilities, but nevertheless a positive environment can be provided. At the same time, we must be careful not to paint children with disabilities with the brush of low expectations, especially for those with learning and mild disabilities. Many students with learning disabilities have the possibility of becoming college- and career-ready, but including those with severe disabilities may be suspect (discussed further in Chapter 7).

Nonetheless, students with learning and mild disabilities will find many aspects of the standards challenging (i.e., synthesizing, analyzing). Mastering complex vocabulary and higher level skills with deficits in reading will be problematic. If students are trying to master basic reading skills, acquiring higher level comprehension skills will be difficult and they will need continued support from teachers. School leaders and special education leaders will have to work together to establish realistic goals, yet this process of adjustment must start with the vision of the CCSS.

Reading is critical for every subject (i.e., math, science, and history), and ascertaining the best reading level at which students can succeed is paramount. Students with disabilities cannot be pushed into text that they cannot read. They will need guided practice and specific, explicit instructions to help them develop skills. Instruction for every class must be designed to meet the needs of the highest and lowest performing students.

We know that modifications made for students with disabilities can frequently benefit the whole class. Most often, students with disabilities are relegated to the lowest levels of Bloom's taxonomy with endless repetition of mindless facts. Even though disabilities are often manifested in reading difficulties, this does not preclude the teaching of higher level skills for those with learning challenges; after all, they most likely attend post-secondary schools. It does mean that schools must work to discover or create reading materials in all subject areas at appropriate levels that also present the reader with disabilities with high-level and thought-provoking questions, choices, and decisions.

All students with disabilities will have an Individualized Education Plan (IEP). School and special education leaders will need to work together to adapt instruction to meet the standards. In the era of the Common Core, IEPs must actually be individualized. It is no longer acceptable for the same set of generic learning goals to show up on the IEP of multiple students in the same class simply as a means of convenience. Special education and school leaders and teachers must work collaboratively to provide:

- appropriate assistive technology;
- evidence-based interventions that work well with students with disabilities;
- instruction and encouragement for teachers to infuse foundational skills into planning, instruction, and assessments; and
- engage and educate parents in the processes and to consider parental opinions honestly and equally.

Applying the Common Core Standards and Solutions

In 2013, 1,300 teachers were surveyed and 28 were interviewed, and the researchers found that teacher's perceptions of the CCSS were noticeable more positively when administrators and school leaders had an open leadership style, including flexibility and assigning importance to teacher input. In this study, it was found that effective leaders share information, and an autocratic style of leadership was discouraged (Hietin, 2014). In *From Common Core Standards to Curriculum: Five Big Ideas*, McTighe and Wiggins (2012) identify principles for teachers that leaders can use as a basis to help their staff implement the CCSS. Leaders must remember to:

- Read through the standards with teachers to assure that they understand what they mean.

- Help teachers understand that the standards is not the curriculum and the curriculum must be developed in collaboration with administrators.

- Provide teachers the means to reach the outcomes, the curriculum and teaching methods that must be developed from the standards.

- Assure teachers that checking off a list of skills cannot be a means to yield the interwoven outcomes "that the Standards envision".

- Assure that teachers analyze the content of the standards related to and identify the essential content of the standards related to goals, overarching understandings, essential questions, and recurring tasks.

- Collaboratively create the new infused curriculum the CCSS will replace.

The CCSS will bring cultural changes of major proportions to schools. To understand cultural change one must understand cultural creation. The people in the organization created a school's culture in order to solve the problems that confronted them on a regular basis (Trice & Beyer, 1993). Over a period of time, those solutions become engrained into how people in the organization behave. Therefore, a leader who simply announces that "things are going to change" seldom gets the desired change.

Cultural change is much more difficult than cultural maintenance, especially if that change is viewed as revolutionary rather than evolutionary as are the changes brought about by the CCSS. Why is that so? Trice and Beyer (1993) describe cultural change as having a duality of purpose—a two-headed dragon, if you will—of creation and destruction. Leaders who ignore that people have good reasons (the destruction of things that have worked in the past) to rebel against cultural change will fight an uphill battle.

Cultural change is uncomfortable, and the only way forward is to become comfortable with discomfort, and that is no easy task. In the era of leadership in the Common Core, leaders must demonstrate themselves that working outside of their own comfort zones is not only possible but also highly rewarding (Trice & Beyer, 1993).

Fullan (2008) believes that "Behaviors change before beliefs." In other words, buy-in is a consequence of results, not a precondition for action. But there is an ethical consideration here as well. Leaders must be keenly knowledgeable of the abilities of their staffs. If a staff member does not already possess the abilities and skills necessary to adopt or adapt to a new philosophy of teaching and learning, then no matter how many belief statements are agreed upon, little actual change is probable or even possible. Therefore, a leader in the era of the CCSS must lead the change in cultural beliefs by providing new experiences for staff that yield tangible, rather than merely hoped for, results in the form of increased student learning for all students.

Connections to Assessment

There are two consortia chosen to develop assessments: the Partnership for the Assessment of Readiness for College and Careers, and the SMARTER Balanced Assessment Consortium (SBAC, 2010). These groups have been assigned to develop comprehensive assessment systems tied to student achievement. These consortia are developing a series of diagnostic, formative, or interim tests to provide ongoing feedback to the school.

Heitin (2014) discussed the heightened need for formative assessment as schools adopt the CCSS. Teachers must learn to adapt and adjust lessons, assessments, and interventions as an ongoing process. As students move toward inquiry and performance task and constructing arguments in the CCSS era, it is noted that the way we use formative assessments will dramatically change. This process is evolving and the adoption of new techniques is a tedious process that will take time.

Formative assessments can make a difference in the implementation of the CCSS. In addition to students' ongoing assessments, teachers will need to perform ongoing self-assessments. CCSS reorganization can only succeed when there is appropriate professional development, staff buy-in, collaborative participation from teachers, and an appropriate curriculum (Rose, 2011). Formative assessments must be planned in order to determine what should be systematically measured, in order to obtain the students' level of knowledge (Popham, 2008). This is especially helpful with ELL students as teachers can find the best way to assess what they actually know, regardless of language barriers.

For students with disabilities, formative assessments are based on their IEPs as these students receive supported interventions. School leaders will need to use creative efforts to help teachers transform their practices using inquiry methods. Just as the vignette mentioned earlier suggests, teachers will need to address formative assessments as part of interventions with CCSS, in order for teachers to help children with disabilities and other populations.

Leaders should assure that:

- special and general teachers have more time to collaborate (Manley & Hawkins, 2013);
- teachers learn to devise formative assessments;
- perform three to five formative assessments during the period that the skill is being taught; as mastery is noted in four to five scores (Manley & Hawkins, 2013); and
- devise rubrics and meet to discuss interventions that show promise and those that do not according to the formative assessments that they performed.

Research-Based Practical Tips and Caveats

Leaders should do the following:

- Collaborate with both special and general educators in order to have an inclusive CCSS curriculum.
- Include teachers in planning and avoid an autocratic leadership style.
- Realize the progression of skills and the different level of implementation for elementary, middle, and high school students.
- Ensure that students with disabilities have specific accommodations and modifications related to their IEP and adapted to CCSS.
- Create, monitor, and use the data from formative assessment systems to accompany the CCSS.
- Create and/or provide quality professional development consistent with CCSS goals and standards.
- Implement schoolwide cultural change with mastery learning as the expectation.

Summary

A School Leader's Guide to Implementing the Common Core: Inclusive Practices for All Students will engage leaders in effective practical applications as they employ critical thinking about problem-solving techniques with teachers. This guide is grounded in best practices from current literature for leaders with applications for staff, teachers, parents, and students. The text is written from a practical perspective targeting building-level and special education leaders. Both special education and general education leaders such as department of instruction personnel, professors of special education, and professors of educational leadership will have input from the text.

As this first chapter began, we read about a conflict. Mrs. Strict, the veteran math teacher, is threatened by the teaching methods that her colleague, Mrs. Adapt, uses to teach Common Core mathematics. When the learning disabilities teacher, Mrs. Strategies, suggests working together with students with learning disabilities, Mrs. Strict sees this as a problem. Teacher conflicts over methodologies and the inevitably end up in the principal's office.

It is, therefore, appropriate that this book began with the role of leadership in the successful implementation of CCSS for all students. Principals will need all of their leadership skills to bring about embraced collaboration between Mrs. Strict and her colleagues. Principals are being asked to change the culture of their institution from success for some to success for all students, and this is a change in how the entire institution believes, sees the future, and acts on those beliefs and that vision of learning for all.

The following chapters will solidly define how UDL and RTI merge. A vignette in each chapter that applies these principles to elementary, middle, and high school youngsters in various environments will provide concrete applications. With the large influx of ESL, ELL, and LEP students in urban settings, the book will address these environments and will expose the reader to circumstances in which to apply the practical situational analysis.

References

About PARCC. (2014). *Partnership for the Assessment of Readiness for College and Careers.* Retrieved from http://www.parcconline.org/about-parcc

About the Standards. (n.d.). *Common Core State Standards initiative.* Retrieved from http://www.corestandards.org/about-the-standards

Ayres, K. M. (2012). Reconciling ecological educational planning with access to the Common Core: Putting the cart before the Horse? A response to Hunt and McDonnell. *Research & Practice for Persons with Severe Disabilities, 37*(3), 153–156.

Courtade, J., Spooner, F., Browder, D., & Jimenez, B. (2012). Seven reasons to promote standards-based instruction for students with severe disabilities: A reply to Ayres, Lowery, Douglas, & Sievers (2011). *Education and Training in Autism and Developmental Disabilities, 47,* 3–13.

Dalley, C. (2012). *Teacher caring, deficit thinking, engagement of students, involvement of parents and the relationships with middle school achievement of at-risk students.* Unpublished dissertation, Department of Education Administration, Leadership and Technology, School of Education, Dowling College, Oakdale, NY.

Dana, N. F., Burns, J. B., & Wolkenhauer, R. (2013). *Inquiring into the Common Core.* Thousand Oaks, CA: Corwin.

Dunaway, M. (2009, August 30). *Leadership: My poor babies.* Retrieved from http://uncceduleaders. ning.com/profiles/blog/leadership-my-poor-babies?context=tag-leadership

Dunkle, C. A. (2012). *Leading the Common Core State Standards: From common sense to common practice.* Thousand Oaks, CA: Corwin.

Education Commission of the States. (2005). *Prisoners of time.* Denver, CO: Education Commission of the States (Original work published 1994, ERIC Document Reproduction Service No. ED48934).

English Language Arts Standards. (n.d.). *Common Core State Standards initiative.* Retrieved from http://www.corestandards.org/ELA-Literacy

Fullan, M. (2008). *The six secrets of change* (Keynote presentation handout). Retrieved from http://www.michaelfullan.ca/images/handouts/2008SixSecretsofChangeKeynoteA4.pdf

Gallup-Education Week Superintendent Panel. (2013, October 7). *Gallup-education week superintendent panel—2013 survey 3 findings.* Retrieved from http://www.gallup.com/services/176777/gallup-education-week-superintendent-panel-2013-survey-findings.aspx

Gamm, S., Elliott, J., Wright Halbert, J. W., Price-Baugh, R., Hall, R., Walston, D., . . . Casserly, M. (2012). *Common Core State Standards and diverse urban students: Using multi-tiered systems of support.* Washington, DC: Council of the Great City Schools. Retrieved from http://www.cgcs.org/domain/87

Haager, D. (2013). The Common Core State Standards and reading: Interpretations and implications for elementary students with learning disabilities. *Learning Disabilities Research & Practice, 28*(1), 5–16.

Heitin, L. (2014). Formative assessment seen as key in Common-Core era. *Education Week, 33*(27), 10–11.

Machiavelli, N. (1532). *The prince [II Principe].* New York: Mentor.

Manley, R. J., & Hawkins, R. J. (2013). *Making the Common Core standards work: Using professional development to build world-class schools.* Thousand Oaks, CA: Corwin.

Mathematics Standards. (n.d.). *Common Core State Standards initiative.* Retrieved from http://www.corestandards.org/Math

McTighe, J., & Wiggins, G. (2012). *From Common Core standards to curriculum: Five big ideas.* Retrieved from http://grantwiggins.files.wordpress.com/2012/09/mctighe_wiggins_final_common_core_standards.pdf

Popham, W. J. (2008). *Transformative assessment.* Alexandra, VA: Association for Supervision and Curriculum Development.

Rose, M. (2011). Something in common: AFT steps up efforts to keep Common Core standards positive and on track. *American Teacher, 96*(1), 12–13.

Scruggs, T. E., Brigham, F. J., & Mastropieri, M. A. (2013). Common Core science standards: Implications for students with learning disabilities. *Learning Disabilities Research & Practice, 28*(1), 49–57.

SMARTER Balanced Assessment Consortium (SBAC). (2010). *Latest news.* Retrieved from http://www.smarterbalanced.org

Trice, H. M., & Beyer, J. M. (1993). *The cultures of work organizations.* Englewood Cliffs, NJ: Prentice Hall.

Ujifusa, A. (2014). Observers put Common-Core rollout under microscope. *Education Week, 33*(28), 19–20.

Understanding the Common Core Standards. (2014, April). Understanding the Common Core standards. *Education Digest, 79*(8), 16–21.

CHAPTER

2

Connecting the Dots to Educational Planning

Keonya Booker and Gloria D. Campbell-Whatley

Principal Concern thought, "The District Superintendent wants all the teachers to use the CCSS by next year. I have a group of resistant teachers who 'have their way of doing things.' What types of trainings can I do with them or what kind of professional development experience can I provide? After all, this is for the children." Upon further reflection, Principal Concern thought, "I also have to think of Mrs. Past, who has been teaching for decades, and she does not want the students with disabilities to be included in anything." A light bulb went off as she thought, "This is not the first time I have tackled the standards, or any other ideas that need to be implemented. I will get everybody onboard. I will call together my assistant principals and start to form collaborative teams. We will begin to look at the data. Mrs. Future is always taking classes even though she has been teaching for years. I will invite her and ask her to rally the other teachers who have been here for a while. Let's see. What other things can I do."

Introduction

General and special education have a number of shared initiatives. This chapter will guide building-level and special education leaders in knowledge related to devising a cohesive and collaborative Common Core curriculum for general and special education teachers. Practitioners will be directed regarding the legalities of the Individuals with Disabilities Education Act (IDEA), the Elementary and Secondary Education Act (ESEA), and ways they combine the two in order to develop standards for all children.

Teaching Teachers How to Use and Infuse the Common Core Standards

The CCSS were developed in response to a growing need for accountability, transparency, and comprehensive educational reform at the state and national levels. The global economy now requires better preparation of American students to compete on an international scale. The United States ranked 21st and 31st in tests of literacy and mathematics, respectively, in comparison to other nations (National Center for Education Statistics, 2015). Beyond the necessity for college and workforce preparation, there was also a concern about students' mobility and the rigor of education for students in underserved areas. The standards were designed to ensure that youth from every part of the country and in all geographical and socioeconomic locales were evaluated on the same achievement domains (National Governors Association Center for Best Practices & Council of Chief State School Officers, 2010). Regardless of whether a child moved from the rural heartland to an urban metropolis, the achievement outcomes should, theoretically, be equivalent.

In the era of the Common Core, states that adopted the standards must consider the enactment of content standards and performance standards. Skinner and Feder (2014) noted that *"content standards* specify what students are expected to know and be able to do … *performance standards* are explicit definitions of what students must know and be able to do to demonstrate proficiency" (p. 7). To borrow a term from research methods, curricula are developed to operationalize or specifically define the standards and the degree of mastery deemed acceptable (Cizek, Bunch, & Koons, 2004). Whereas the Common Core may be prescriptive in content, the instructional decisions for how information is presented to students remains at district and classroom levels. For this reason, it is important to provide teachers with the tools, skills, and instruments to educate students in creative and collaborative ways.

In the absence of a specified program of study, teachers can use the spirit of the Common Core to develop and share resources that can support student mastery of grade-level learning. Because the standards denote what students should know and be able to exhibit by the end of the year, teachers will need to have a blueprint in order to build a solid foundation for proficiency. Concepts cannot be presented in isolation, but there should be ample time allotted to develop and deepen curricular objectives. Tools for classroom application come in a range of areas, including the development of critical thinking skills, problem solving, and being a good consumer of research. As an example, teachers will need help with content integration, showing how literacy relates to social studies or how integers connect to social geography. Furthermore, the standards provide a seamless transition from grade to grade. If a third-grade teacher knows the standards from second grade, he can build upon those concepts without having to repeat information unnecessarily and missing critical instructional time for original ideas. By using the content standards from a previous grade, the teacher can create a stronger base for new learning to take place.

IDEA and ESEA: Driving at the Intersection

The ESEA of 1965 was borne out of an appeal to provide equal educational opportunities for all American schoolchildren. The promise of educational reform to some of the most poverty-stricken and underserved parts of the country gave hope in closing the achievement gap for underserved youth (Wirtz & Chalfant, 1965). Title I schools were created to provide children in poor urban and rural areas access to equal education as that of their suburban counterparts. In 2001, the ESEA was amended and reauthorized by the G.W. Bush administration as the No Child Left Behind Act (NCLB). Skinner and Feder (2014) report that NCLB required states participating in ESEA Title I-A to develop, adopt content, and align assessments for (a) mathematics and reading in grades 3–8 and for at least one grade for 10–12 by the end of the 2005–2006 school year; and (b) science for at least three levels for grades 3–5, 6–9, and 10–12 by the end of the 2007–2008 school year.

The NCLB was touted as a way to focus on more stringent accountability methods, primarily by way of standardized testing and statewide assessments. Buzzwords like *data-proven teaching methods, high-quality teachers,* and *adequate yearly progress* flooded the national debate on student learning and achievement. What followed was an inordinate amount of stress, pressure, and testing "frenzy" that left districts with unprecedented school closures, parents and students with elevated distress from high-stakes assessments, and lower teacher morale (Hill & Barth, 2004). The paradox of NCLB is that the communities that were to be the beneficiaries of sweeping reform were now disproportionally affected by the unintended consequences of overregulation. These consequences included a disconnection with the local community, charter schools without oversight, and high levels of school withdrawal for certain populations of students from low socioeconomic communities.

The goals of ESEA and NCLB were laudable. The plan was to ensure a rigorous and equitable schooling experience for all American youth, regardless of background, geographical locale, or life circumstance. If a state received Title I funding, it was "required to bring all students to a proficient reading and mathematics level by 2014" (Cortiella, 2006, p. 6). For a certain group of students, however, the provisions of these two legislative acts would need to be revisited. In 2004, Bush reauthorized the IDEA, allowing for increased access to the general education curriculum for students with disabilities. The premise of IDEA was to uphold processes involving children and their families in the general curriculum. These protections would ensure that youth with disabilities were making progress toward specified educational objectives and performance targets. A cornerstone of IDEA, the IEP, denotes a student's present level of performance, annual goals, and any supplemental aids, supports, or services needed to assist them in maximum involvement and access to the general education curriculum (Konrad et al., 2014).

It is a legal document with planning and assessment implications for teachers, administrators, and support personnel.

As aforementioned, NCLB required states to develop challenging academic standards for content and achievement in mathematics, literacy, and (by 2008) science. As Karger (2005) maintains, "The development of standards is thus a point of intersection for the two statutes: IDEA requires that students with disabilities have access to the general education curriculum, according to their individualized needs, while NCLB helps to define and raise the level of the general education curriculum" (p. 13). Noticeably, the existence of the standards facilitates the operationalizing of the curricula. The line of reasoning becomes that the law necessitates a high-quality general education curriculum for all students, regardless of demographic differences. If supported access to the general education curriculum is a mandate of IDEA, then children with disabilities reap the benefits of a superior educational experience by their sustained connection to the general education classroom.

Legal Issues

There are two main areas where the legality of these policies applies to the work of school and special education leaders. IDEA requires that students with disabilities be educated in the least restrictive environment. This provision means every effort should be made for children with disabilities to maintain access within the general education curriculum. Removal from the general education classroom is a last resort, unless the nature of the disability requires a different placement. The composition of the IEP team is another area where a preference for the student to remain engaged with the general education environment is present. IDEA requires that the IEP team should consist of one special education teacher and one general education teacher. School leaders will need to comply with legal directives and work with special education faculty to support the general education placements of students with disabilities, as deemed appropriate by the IEP team.

The second domain where legal issues arise is in the assessment arena. Students with disabilities are expected to participate in the state and district assessments as predicated by NCLB. Grade-level state assessments are to be aligned with the academic content standards adopted by each state education agency. Subgroup reporting of racial, ethnic, and disabilities categories is required to determine adequate yearly progress and continuous improvement of student learning. To facilitate participation in statewide assessments, students with an IEP who require testing accommodations must be allowed to use these adaptations. Accommodations such as presentation, response, timing, and setting (Cortiella, 2006) should be adhered to so that assessments are valid indicators of what the child knows and not necessarily the extent of the disability. These accommodations allow for broad participation in the general education curriculum while maintaining students' rights to a rigorous educational experience (Thompson, Morse, Sharpe, & Hall, 2005). For students with severe cognitive disabilities, alternate assessments can be used as a measure of learning against state standards. Again, the IEP team would make the determination of the student's fitness to participate in the assessment process.

Merging Concepts

Both IDEA and NCLB compel first-rate individualized instruction for all American schoolchildren. Because of this condition, lawmakers call for the employment of "highly qualified teachers." According to the legislation, *highly effective* teachers have undergone training which includes meticulous undergraduate academic work, state certification and licensure, ongoing professional development (PD), and regular observations by school leaders. With respect to subject matter expertise, NCLB and IDEA mandate that special education teachers of core academic subjects be well versed in both core academic domains and special education principles and practices.

In addition to the directive for well-trained instructional personnel, NCLB expects PD for both regular education and special education teachers. This PD can take the form of pedagogical activities on learning styles, dispositions of students with disabilities, and assistive technology. One of the most significant parts of NCLB's continuing education charge is the emphasis on collaboration between general education and special education teachers. As many of these staff members will be working in tandem with one another on child study, IEP, and transition teams, engaging in discussions about best practices is beneficial for all teachers and students. Regular education teachers can share strategies for ways to connect with the general education curriculum, while special education teachers can communicate the distinctive needs of students with disabilities and how best to reach these youth.

School Environmental Challenges and Solutions: Smoothing Rough Places

In the age of accountability, school administrators will be expected to take on a leadership role in instruction and assessment. School leaders must have knowledge of pertinent legislation and legal mandates that affect their student body, instructional staff, and the larger school population. As the opening vignette demonstrates, school leaders may encounter confusion, resistance, or apathy about the tenets of ESEA, NCLB, and IDEA. As the CCSS are an outgrowth of these laws, leaders will need to be proactive in communicating impending changes. In this section, attention will be paid to addressing these challenges in a collaborative and meaningful way.

School-Based Leaders

School-based leaders are responsible for creating a vision for the school community's adoption of the CCSS. Part of establishing a vision is engaging essential stakeholders in the process of change. The entire school community (i.e., students, teachers, parents and families, business leaders, and elected officials) will be responsible for carrying out these efforts, and some will be indirect beneficiaries of the outcomes. Active discussions on issues such as capacity building, training and support, and coordination of resources will reinforce the management of state and national policies.

Research shows that teacher "buy-in" is an integral part of the success of any novel schoolwide initiative (Smith & Ingersoll, 2004). Ongoing communication will be required to ensure that teachers understand the CCSS, are aware of how to implement them, and remain committed to their instructional roles. Surveys, workshops, and general open-door policies are ways school leaders can promote an environment of understanding and engagement while the CCSS are being applied. As conversations occur, school leaders will want to take note of those teachers, such as Mrs. Future in the opening vignette, who are poised to take a leadership role at the staff level.

Darling-Hammond, Wei, Andree, Richardson, and Orphanos (2009) posit four characteristics of PD that leadership should consider when designing effective training for teachers:

- PD activities should be intensive, continuous, and based on empirical practice. Self-reports of teachers indicate that they want more time to apply information gained during PD endeavors and longer intervals between sessions to reflect on how to put the strategies into practice. Part of the challenge is finding enough time during the standard workweek, or even full school semester, for continuing education. Marrongelle, Sztajn, and Smith (2013) contend, "using a variety of delivery mechanisms to make PD available to teachers assures that such initiatives fit a myriad of teacher schedules and working conditions" (p. 206). School leaders must display a willingness to provide these alternative options and recognize those who choose to take advantage of the range of opportunities available to them.

- In these PD sessions, teachers must focus on how the curriculum relates to student learning outcomes (Darling-Hammond et al., 2009). Change brings anxiety and reluctance, so having teachers walk a mile in the shoes of their pupils will give them greater confidence in teaching the curriculum that aligns with the standards. PD can offer teachers a chance to engage in learning the content themselves, watching demonstrations of instructional strategies, and reviewing student work samples for trends in the data. When teachers can anticipate problems and errors, they will better plan their instruction in the future. Teachers can also be more responsive to student needs on an academic and motivational level.

- Darling-Hammond et al. (2009) state that PD should also ensure alignment with school improvement goals and reform. In the case of the CCSS, PD activities should come into line with the state curriculum. Administrators from the district can offer detailed workshops and planning sessions for teachers to support a deeper understanding of the standards and how they relate to working with students with disabilities, from underserved populations, or with other learning challenges. If a state education agency has adopted the standards, then there should be monies set aside for the preparation of instructional staff (Reeves, 2012).

- PD must include a relationship-building component. Whether by informal coaching, tutoring, or through more sustained and formalized mechanisms, such as induction models (Wang, Odell, & Schwille, 2008), school-based leaders must support teaching staff by encouraging collaboration among special and general educational teachers. Teaching is an interpersonal activity, and instructional staff need the time, space, and encouragement to work together planning lessons, discussing promising teaching tools, and reflecting on the move to the Common Core. While it is useful to start with grade-level staff, teachers can work in larger groups as well to facilitate ideas across grades and placements. School leaders and district officials may also connect with local universities to engage teacher education faculty around issues with CCSS instruction and assessment. As college faculty are charged with disseminating and also creating knowledge in the form of original research and evaluation studies, this group is poised to be on the front line of innovative work in the area of the standards and scaled-up PD.

Special Education Leaders

It is important that special education leaders support grade-level staff with appropriate PD activities and identifying resources (both human and fiscal) that can support additional training for special education personnel. The CCSS leaders do not stipulate teaching methods, only outcomes, so special education leaders will need to support both general and special education teachers with instructional techniques to reach all students. As Konrad et al. (2014) state, "The standards are intentionally broad and do not represent the detail required for lesson planning. Therefore, standards must be deconstructed or unpacked before instruction is planned" (p. 77). Special education leaders can convene groups of specialists and generalists to establish knowledge, reasoning, skill, and product targets. When planning, attention must be given to considering evidence of student learning, timing of skill development, and ordering of lessons. Special education leaders can supply teachers with steering questions to guide this work.

Special education leaders, with a deep knowledge of characteristics, can also be of support when helping teachers work with particular groups of students with disabilities. For example, students with processing disabilities, for example, autism, will need help in managing executive functioning (i.e., organization, time management, planning, and impulsivity). Special education leaders can show teachers how to reduce stress and provide structure for students (Constable, Grossi, Moniz, & Ryan, 2013). As another example, the CCSS include outcomes such as speaking, listening, and writing. In response to these requirements, teachers must reflect on ways to support students in their development of expressive and receptive language skills. Special education leaders will need to assist teachers in incorporating research-proven strategies, such as prompting, visual support, and peer-mediated instruction, to reach these students (Carter, Cushing, Clark, & Kennedy, 2005). It should be mentioned here that these tools are not relegated only to special education teachers but are useful applications for all teachers and for all students.

The IEP is a blueprint for showing where the child is currently functioning and where they need to go with the help of instructional supports, technology, and other assistive devices. The present level of performance and annual goals should be aligned with grade-level standards which are determined by the Common Core statutes (Konrad et al., 2014). Special education leaders may work together with the full team to ensure IEP annual goals and learning targets are explicit and convey clear, observable, and measurable evidence of student learning. During these meetings, leadership will also be available to help teachers use appropriate messaging when communicating with parents and families.

The final area in which special education leaders will be vital is in accommodations. Teachers must be aware of important special education practices such as Universal Design for Learning (UDL) (discussed further in Chapter 8). In UDL, teachers proactively think about how information is presented and if knowledge can be demonstrated in a multitude of ways (Pisha & Coyne, 2001). When instructional staff use UDL, a priority is placed on motivation, learning styles, and alternative measures of engagement. Special education leaders can help teachers review classroom routines, define student learning outcomes, and plan for specific adaptations such as planners, dictation, or word banks (Kurth, 2013). Again, collaboration among general and special education teachers is key. Evaluation of the adaptations can be a joint process between classroom teachers, school leaders, and special education leaders.

Teachers, special educators, and school leaders must work together to ensure a positive learning experience for all students. This collaboration includes open communication, positive attitudes, and a willingness to ask for assistance when necessary. All members of the school community are critical stakeholders, and their voices should be heard when engaging vested groups in discussions pertaining to the CCSS.

Applying the Common Core Standards and Solutions

School leaders and instructional personnel are encouraged to adopt the following practices as it relates to educational planning for all children, regardless of disability category. In particular, school leaders will need to:

■ Stay abreast of important changes to national and state legislation associated with the CCSS, NCLB, and the IDEA. At the time of this writing, the U.S. Senate Health, Education, Labor and Pensions Committee had unanimously approved the Every Child Achieves Act, a reauthorization of NCLB which would reduce an overreliance on high-stakes testing and increase funding for research-based innovative practices in P–12 education. When, and if, new legislation goes into effect, school leaders can request that representatives from the state provide in-service training opportunities for instructional personnel.

■ Work with state education officials to develop a delivery chain of pertinent information regarding the CCSS (Achieve and U.S. Education Delivery Institute, 2012). Messaging should "define the issue, outline the problem, and explain the solution" (p. 4.8). These communications will change slightly based on the intended stakeholder group, but having a unifying theme will help the various populations understand the expectations coming from the state education agency as well as school leadership.

■ Draw on the knowledge, skills, and strengths of the teaching staff and create grade-level leadership teams that can disseminate vital information to their colleagues. School leaders can leverage the experience and training of instructional staff to collaborate on standards reform as it relates to the school's mission and goals. Administrators should be willing to listen, observe, and seek feedback from all members of the community, but especially the teachers who are on the front line of delivering the CCSS.

■ Use data in all forms (statewide testing results, adequate yearly progress, The Partnership for Assessment of Readiness for College and Careers [PARCC], and Smarter Balanced Assessment Consortium [SBAC] scores in formative and summative assessments). There is an old saying in leadership and management that "what gets monitored gets done." School leaders should develop clearly defined procedures for evaluating and observing teachers' adoption and implementation of the CCSS. As a reminder, leaders will want to view the data as dynamic points of information, not static indicators of student or teacher worth.

- Develop and maintain positive relationships with parents, families, and community members. School leaders may work with special education leaders and grade-level instructional leaders to ensure multiple perspectives are considered when determining methods, frequency, and content of the communications.

As previously mentioned, the CCSS are not curricula. Thus, classroom teachers should use originality, creativity, and evidence-based practices when engaged in educational planning and lesson development. Teachers can:

- Attend various PD opportunities offered by building-level, district, and state personnel. Learning does not end with the conferral of a degree. Teachers should constantly seek out ways to develop their skills and reflect on their role in the classroom (Guskey, 2002).

- Collaborate with other grade-level or subject-area colleagues to deepen their understanding about how the standards impact student learning outcomes and instructional planning. Carve out time during the workday or work-week to connect with others in the school community to share ideas and get feedback. During these continuing education activities, teachers can find like-minded people who may offer useful teaching and assessment strategies. Learning communities are an excellent way to monitor student performance and set goals as a grade-level or subject-area team (forms and suggestions in Chapter 9).

- Use principles such as UDL to provide students with different ways to receive and express content knowledge (discussed in-depth in Chapter 8). Adapting your teaching approach speaks to your understanding of students' need for mastery, engagement, and competence in the learning domain.

- Consider taking a leadership role at the grade or building level. If there are opportunities for governance, use your skills and abilities to teach colleagues ways to apply the standards in a methods that reaches all schoolchildren.

Connections to Assessment

Educational reform in the United States in the last two decades uses a system of standardized test accompanied by rewards and sanctions for teachers and students and has moved from state testing for accountability to federally mandated systems (Deville & Chalhoub-Deville, 2011). A Nation at Risk's Goals 2000: Educate America Act (1994), the first major reform that shifted funding from the state to the federal government, established a set of national performance standards; the accompanied assessment system was developed by the National Council on Educational Standards and Testing in 1992. The accountability system in ESEA and reauthorized in NCLB produced measures of performance that (a) improved teacher quality, (b) rebuilt schools that were failing, (c) began the school report card system, and (d) set discipline codes. Recently, *A Blueprint for Reform* (2010) ushered the CCSS which provided a focus on curricula. The National Governor's Association and the Council of Chief State School Officers guidelines show that 85 percent of the standards come from CCSS and consequently states must reconcile NCLB and CCSS. There are now many new assessment challenges with CCSS that had been worked through with NCLB.

These new constructs guide classroom instruction, curriculum-based and formative assessments, and PD. Testing accommodations and modifications for students with disabilities and English language leaner (ELL) students also presents special challenges. Murphy and Smith (2013) point out that the language of CCSS may be problematic (i.e., the assessment of *range*). Within the standards, the area of variation between upper and lower limits on a particular scale presents a threat to assessment. For example, judging and observing measures of writing standards where *range* could be applied might differ with the purpose of a particular written piece or the integration of reading within a writing assignment, as well as various writing situations within the classroom; all affect the validity of assessment when judging *range*.

Within the consortium-based testing system of CSSS, SBAC and PARCC share benchmarks and cut-off scores, as well as several other common features such as (a) online testing, (b) summative and course-embedded (formative) assessments, (c) achievement information, (d) comparison scores, and (e) adaptations for ELLs and students with disabilities.

Willhoft (2013) states that school leaders will need to prepare for the next generation of assessments. Schools will need sufficient hardware to meet the new technology requirements and the heavy use of computers for instruction and assessments. SBAC will require end-of-year summative assessments within a 12-week window of administration during the last months of school, in multiple testing sessions (Doorey, 2014; Wilhoft, 2013). A number of sample items that include performance task, multistep problems, and classroom-based activities are provided on the SBAC website (http://sbac.portal.airast.org/practice-test/).

PARCC and SBAC has a number of features; for example, the computer-assisted responses allow for individualized assessments; that is, question difficulty will be adjusted if the student has too many incorrect responses. Moreover, the test will be automatically scored and feedback provided to teachers and students.

By spring of 2015, PARCC states will have administered the test to grades 3–11, and SBAC will have administered them in grades 3–8 and 11 (9 and 10 in some states) (Dorrey, 2014). The complete test takes 7–10 hours to administer. PARCC has nine testing sessions across two testing windows. The performance-based English/language arts (E/LA) will have three sessions, while the mathematics assessments will consist of two sessions; both will occur after

75 percent of instruction. The end-of-year assessment will have a four-week window with E/LA and mathematics consisting of two sessions each; both occurring after 90 percent of instruction. These assessments will be partially machine-scored.

There are online materials that support assessment. Achieve the Core (www.achievethecore.org) offers core aligned lessons, and Engage (www.engageny.org) contains curriculum models, assessments, videos, and resources for families. These websites help teachers and school leaders demonstrate imaginative and innovative ways to prepare students for the assessments, for example, types of questioning, inquiries, and real-world problems that can be introduced into the classroom setting. Creative Commons (www.creativecommons.org) provides an interactive website where teachers and leaders converse with people who have created innovative modules and lessons (Riley, 2013).

A large part of assessment for CCSS is the use of formative assessments (discussed further in Chapters 3 and 9). Connecting high-stakes summative assessments with in-class formative assessments creates a powerful system of instruction. Large-scale test focuses on the summative skills, knowledge, and information a student has learned, while formative assessments focus on student learning in increments and drive instruction so that what the student has learned—or has not learned—is measured. Formative assessments have more impact on day-to-day academic growth, while large-scale assessments determine overall curriculum content and delivery (Ainsworth & Viegut, 2006). Formative assessments should be aligned to the large-scale assessment and offer a predictive value of how the students will perform on high-stakes CCSS test. Both are necessary for complete and accurate measures of a student's academic ability. Formative assessments should be designed by both school leaders and teacher teams throughout the year (Ainsworth & Viegut, 2006). Leaders will need to ensure that teachers are aware of the strengths that formative measures bring to assessments to improve the quality of instruction. They must change schedules to encourage grade-level meetings and use other techniques to effectively plan collaborative measures for implementation.

Research-Based Practical Tips and Caveats

- School leaders must stay abreast of all the changes in legislature and legal mandates and engage the school community in change and development while encouraging teacher buy-in.

- School leaders must use a number of delivery systems to promote PD. It is important for teachers to learn to instruct students in a creative collaborative manner.

- PD should be continuous and infused with empirical practices and align with school improvement plan.

- School leaders should encourage collaboration and team building.

- Special education leaders must ensure that general educators are operating in the realm of legalities for special education students.

- Both special and general education leaders must be aware of the nuances of PARCC and SBAC and the technological demands. Summative as well as formative assessments are important to the implementation of CCSS assessments. All data should be used to make decisions about curriculum and students.

- NCLB, IDEA, and CCSS are to be used in unison. Each offers essentials for instruction and assessment.

Summary

The United States has had a number of reform movements from time to time and school, district, and special education leaders have the onus to ensure appropriate administration of the standards with varied populations of teachers and students, while helping parents to understand the new commitments. Because we have had so many reforms, many teachers have become resistant, as the vignette demonstrates. As we started this chapter, we were looking into the mind of a principal, Mrs. Concern, who has received the "request" from the superintendent that all teachers use the CCSS by the next year. She knows that she has some go-getters who will jump onboard (maybe too quickly) and some who will be resistant.

Leaders will need to become motivators as they form teams, find teacher leaders, and involve assistant principals to help implement the standards. Clearly, Principal Concern has a significant problem.

There are many school leaders who are experiencing the same dilemma as the scenario in the vignette. There will be teachers in the school willing and ready to implement the standards even though they are not prepared, and others who are not ready to implement even with preparation. Other situations to consider include instruction and assessment of students with disabilities, ELLs, and other populations of students who differ. No matter the conflict, the CCSS are here and they must be unpacked and infused into the curriculum. Powerful PD is about efficacy, first in the PD itself and then creating that efficacy in the teachers.

Meaningful PD brings about a change in participants' behavior that improves their performance and, as an effect, their results. Meaningful PD is measurable and brings more value to the professional lives of those who participated in it.

The implementation of CCSS will mean changes not only in instruction but in the way we assess students. The CCSS administrations will be computerized for both SBAC and PARCC, so students and teachers will need to become familiar not only with the test but the manner in which the test is given. To help prepare teachers, PD may include several foci: (a) technology, (b) students with disabilities, (c) ELLs, and (d) summative and formative assessments. The sessions should also be interspersed with current legislation and legalities.

Special and general education leaders alike can work collaboratively to implement CCSS. Implementation depends on strong collaborative teamwork— teamwork that is powerful and meaningful.

References

Achieve and U.S. Education Delivery Institute. (2012). *Implementing Common Core State Standards and assessments.* Washington, DC: U.S. Education Delivery Institute.

Ainsworth, L., & Viegut, D. (2006). *Common formative assessments: How to connect standards-based instruction and assessment.* Thousand Oaks, CA: Corwin Press.

Bambrick-Santoyo, P. (2014, March 1). Assessments can help Common Core teaching. *Phi Delta Kappan, 95*(6), 70–71.

Carter, E. W., Cushing, L. S., Clark, N. M., & Kennedy, C. H. (2005). Effects of peer support interventions on students' access to the general curriculum and social interventions. *Research and Practice for Persons with Severe Disabilities, 30*(1), 15–25.

Cizek, G. J., Bunch, M. B., & Koons, H. (2004). Setting performance standards: Contemporary methods. *Educational Measurement: Issues and Practice, 23*(4), 31–50.

Constable, S., Grossi, B., Moniz, A., & Ryan, L. (2013). Meeting the Common Core State Standards for students with autism: The challenge for educators. *Teaching Exceptional Children, 45*(3), 6–13.

Cortiella, C. (2006). *NCLB and IDEA: What parents of students with disabilities need to know and do?* Minneapolis, MN: University of Minnesota, National Center on Educational Outcomes.

Darling-Hammond, L., Wei, R. C., Andree, A., Richardson, N., & Orphanos, S. (2009). *Professional learning in the learning profession: A status report on teacher development in the United States and abroad.* Dallas, TX: National Staff Development Council.

Deville, C., & Chalhoub-Deville, M. (2011, January 1). Accountability-assessment under No Child Left Behind: Agenda, practice, and future. *Language Testing, 28*(3), 307–321.

Domina, T., Ghosh-Dastidar, B., & Tienda, M. (2010, January 1). Students left behind: Measuring 10th to 12th grade student persistence rates in Texas high schools. *Educational Evaluation and Policy Analysis, 32*(2), 324–346.

Doorey, N. (2014). The Common Core assessments: What you need to know. *Educational Leadership, 71*(6), 57–60.

EBSCO. (2013). Pilot testing Common Core assessments. *District Administration, 49*(5), 18.

Furgol, K., Ho, A., & Zimmerman, D. (2010, January 1). Estimating trends from censored assessment data under No Child Left Behind. *Educational and Psychological Measurement, 70*(5), 760–776.

Goals 2000: Educate America Act of 1994. Pub. L. No. 103–227, 108 Stat. 125 (1994).

Guskey, T. R. (2002). Does it make a difference? Evaluating professional development. *Educational Leadership, 59*(6), 45–51.

Hill, D. M., & Barth, M. (2004). NCLB and teacher retention: Who will turn out the lights? *Education and the Law, 16*(2–3), 173–181.

Karger, J. (2005). *Access to the general education curriculum for students with disabilities: A discussion of the interrelationship between IDEA'04 and NCLB.* Wakefield, MA: National Center on Accessing the General Curriculum.

Konrad, M., Keesey, S., Ressa, V. A., Alexeeff, M., Chan, P. E., & Peters, M. T. (2014). Setting clear learning targets to guide instruction for all students. *Intervention in School and Clinic, 50*(2), 76–85.

Kurth, J. A. (2013). A unit-based approach to adaptations in inclusive classrooms. *Teaching Exceptional Children, 46*(2), 34–43.

Marrongelle, K., Sztajn, P., & Smith, M. (2013). Scaling up professional development in an era of common state standards. *Journal of Teacher Education, 64*(3), 202–211.

Murphy, S., & Smith, M. A. (2013, September 1). Assessment challenges in the Common Core era. *English Journal, 103*(1), 104.

National Association for Music Education. (2013, January 1). New paper examines link between Common Core standards, curriculum, and assessments. *Teaching Music, 20*(4), 3.

National Center for Education Statistics. (2015). *School composition and the Black–White achievement gap.* Retrieved from https://nces.ed.gov

National Governors Association Center for Best Practices & Council of Chief State School Officers. (2010). *Common Core State Standards.* Washington, DC: National Governors Association Center for Best Practices, Council of Chief State School.

Pisha, B., & Coyne, P. (2001). Smart from the start: The promise of Universal Design for Learning. *Remedial and Special Education, 22*(4), 197–203.

Reeves, D. B. (2012). *Transforming professional development into student results.* Alexandria, VA: Association for Supervision and Curriculum Development.

Riley, C. (2013). The Common Core, aligned assessments and the 21st-century classroom: Lessons learned from educators. *Techniques: Connecting Education & Careers, 88*(8), 24–28.

Saunders, A. F., Spooner, F., Browder, D., Wakeman, S., & Lee, A. (2013). Teaching the Common Core in English language arts to student with severe disabilities. *Teaching Exceptional Children, 46*(2), 22–33.

Skinner, R. R., & Feder, J. (2014). *Common Core State Standards and assessments: Background and issues.* Washington, DC: Congressional Research Service.

Smith, T. M., & Ingersoll, R. M. (2004). What are the effects of induction and mentoring on beginning teacher turnover? *American Educational Research Journal, 41*(3), 681–714.

Thompson, S. J., Morse, A. B., Sharpe, M., & Hall, S. (2005). *Accommodations manual: How to select, administer, and evaluate use of accommodations and assessment for students with disabilities.* Washington, DC: Council for Chief State School Officers.

U.S. Department of Education. (2010). *U.S. Department of Education, office of planning, evaluation and policy development, ESEA blueprint for reform.* Washington, DC: U.S. Department of Education.

Wang, J., Odell, S., & Schwille, S. (2008). Effects of teacher induction on beginning teachers' teaching: A critical review. *Journal of Teacher Education, 59*(2), 132–152.

Willhoft, J. (2013). The Common Core and next-generation assessments: Preparing students for CTE. *Techniques: Connecting Education & Careers, 88*(4), 38.

Wirtz, M. A., & Chalfant, J. C. (1965). Elementary and Secondary Education Act: Implications for handicapped children. *Exceptional Children, 32*(3), 139–146.

CHAPTER

3

Data-Driven Formal and Informal Measures

Chuang Wang, Dawson R. Hancock, and Gloria D. Campbell-Whatley

Mrs. Driven, the assistant principal, was in charge of collecting and analyzing the data for students. She now has data, charts, and diagrams in written and digital form. She was sitting in Principal Collection's office asking him, "I have all this data, now what do I do?" The principal began to speak about the importance of teamwork and collaboration. He said, "Let's get some grade level teams together to examine the data. We need to find out what kind of informal measures teachers are using, especially to examine students whose growth may be in smaller increments and make sure that our measures connect to what we are teaching in class. Also, the growing achievement gap needs to be discussed in our teams."

Introduction

This chapter outlines informal, formal, quantitative, and qualitative measures used to examine the schools' progress toward CCSS and how that data can be used to improve the scores of students with and without disabilities and those at risk. Ideas will be provided to lessen the achievement gap for students with disabilities. Additionally, this chapter will connect teaching to assessment practices. Finally, a walkthrough will be provided for school leaders to evaluate teachers in regard to the implementation of the standards.

Formal and Informal Measures

The U.S. federal government has funded two state-led consortia to develop assessments that provide meaningful feedback to teachers and administrators in the states that have adopted the CCSS. These two consortia are Partnership for Assessment of Readiness for College and Career (PARCC) and the Smarter Balanced Assessment Consortium (SBAC). Each state has the freedom to choose the tests from one of the two consortia. However, a state will not be able to influence decisions about assessment design, cost, or field testing until it selects which consortium to use. The following is a review of similarities and differences between the two consortia. Understanding how CCSS are assessed contributes to ensuring that student achievement is comparable across states as well as providing information about how well the instruction based on the CCSS is implemented in each state.

Formal Measures: PARCC versus SBAC

SBAC is managed by the Department of Education in Washington state, whereas PARCC is managed by an independent non-profit organization led by governors and corporate leaders (Porter-Magee, O'Leary, & Partin, 2011). Both consortia are developing computer-administered tests in order to reduce the costs of grading and enhance the validity of the scores. Recent technological advances have made it possible for automated scoring to grade written or spoken responses (e.g., short essays, short text answers to content questions, spoken responses) and mathematical problems in textual, graphical, and numeric formats (Williamson et al., 2010). Both consortia will use a combination of automated scoring and teacher scoring to grade student responses. SBAC is developing computer-adapted tests where the computer will automatically present a test item adapted to the student's ability level based upon the answers given. PARCC, however, is not developing computer-adapted tests but simply will administer the tests on the computer.

SBAC will provide a summative assessment to measure performance tasks where students will complete one task in reading, one task in writing, and two tasks in mathematics. SBAC will also provide computer-adaptive assessments that consist of approximately 40–65 questions for each content area. The computer-adaptive assessments will include selected-response, constructed-response, and technology-enhanced items. SBAC will also allow students to retake the computer-adaptive assessments if they are not satisfied with their performance. The students will work on a new set of items in the same content area and use the higher score in the two assessments.

PARCC is developing both performance-based and end-of-year assessments. Performance-based assessments are mainly for grades 3–8, whereas summative end-of-year assessments will be developed for all grade levels, and the results of these assessments will determine the end-of-year summative assessments. In English language arts, the performance-based assessments will require students to write effectively when analyzing texts. In mathematics, students will be asked to apply the content knowledge and skills learned throughout the year. In addition, PARCC is developing listening and speaking assessments that will be scored by teachers using a common rubric.

Both PARCC and SBAC will use standardized scores and level scores to report student performance on CCSS, practices similar to current state-mandated tests. However, most educators believe that CCSS have established higher expectations for students. The standardized scores from SBAC will range from 2,300 to 2,800. Based upon a field test in 21 states, the distribution of students who reached each of the four levels is revealed in Table 3.1 (Smarter Balanced Assessment Consortium, 2014) in which students are considered "at the grade level" if they reach Level III or higher.

Informal Measures

Both consortia are committed to designing formative assessments to guide instruction by measuring student progress toward mastery of the CCSS and by identifying the learning gaps. Therefore, CCSS assessments may be used to provide teacher feedback about their students' learning processes. Moreover, the computer-adaptive tests, which will be provided by SBAC, will adjust the difficulty of questions based on student responses and provide a uniquely tailored set of items for each student. These adaptive assessments will not only provide accurate measures of student progress but also give teachers richer information about individual student's strengths and weaknesses according to the CCSS (Willhoft, 2012). PARCC is currently working with its governing states to make a decision about the diagnostic tests to be administered at the beginning of each academic year. These diagnostic tests may be administered to help teachers identify knowledge and skills that students did not master in their previous academic year and to identify students who may benefit from enrichment. PARCC has not decided whether these diagnostic tests will be aligned to the grade-level standards or the highest-priority standards required by the previous grade. These tests may also be a combination of the grade-level standards and the highest-priority standards (Porter-Magee et al., 2011). To help teachers

Table 3.1 Estimated Percentages of Students Scoring at Each Achievement Level (Grades 3–8 and 11)

	Mathematics							*English Language Arts/Literacy*						
Grade Level	3	4	5	6	7	8	11	3	4	5	6	7	8	11
I	32	27	35	35	36	38	40	35	37	33	30	34	28	28
II	29	36	32	32	31	30	27	27	22	23	29	28	31	31
III	27	24	18	19	20	19	22	20	23	29	30	30	32	30
IV	12	13	15	14	13	13	11	18	18	15	11	8	9	11

use the data from CCSS assessments for instructional purposes, PARCC will provide teachers with an online score-training tool. Furthermore, PARCC will make mid-year assessments available. Teachers may use these as formative assessments to obtain information about how well their students have mastered the essential skills required by the CCSS. Teachers may also use these assessments to expose students to the types of performance tasks and better prepare them to encounter the end-of-year assessment. Moreover, PARCC will create formative assessments for students in grades K–2 so that teachers may use them to monitor their students' progress toward mastery of content knowledge and skills in these early grades.

Like most assessments of student performance, CCSS assessments will attempt to measure student cognitive thinking, critical and reasoning skills, and the application of knowledge to solve realistic and meaningful problems (Lane, 2010). These high-level thinking skills should be based on factual and procedural knowledge—both important components of a comprehensive education. According to Bloom and Krathwohl's (1956) Taxonomy and Bloom's Revised Taxonomy (Anderson & Krathwohl, 2001), the abilities to apply, analyze, synthesize, and evaluate are considered higher skills in comparison to the abilities to know and comprehend. The CCSS seem to follow a general progression along Bloom's Taxonomy through grade levels with lower elementary grade standards focused more on knowledge and comprehension and higher grade levels focused on application, analysis, synthesis, and evaluation. CCSS assessments are designed to use authentic examples in which students are asked to perform real-world tasks that demonstrate meaningful application of the knowledge and skills learned in the classroom. This should motivate students and facilitate the development of self-regulated learning skills through metacognition (Zimmerman, 2000).

With computer-administered assessments, teachers and students will receive the student performance scores much sooner than they currently receive. In many states, students must wait nearly four months to receive their final results on the state-mandated tests (Porter-Magee et al., 2011). On the contrary, computer-administered assessments can provide students feedback about their performance instantaneously, and the consortia have promised to deliver the test results in a few weeks (Willhoft, 2012). With efficient assessment of the CCSS, automated scoring may make it possible for schools to periodically review student progress to make sure they stay on the path to success and to inform teachers so that they can make adjustments in their instruction, if necessary. Automated scoring may provide scores more quickly and consistently and also reduce the cost of grading in comparison to the use of human graders. Both the availability and acceptance of automated scoring may make longitudinal analyses of student outcomes more accessible. Researchers and teachers may be able to use these longitudinal and consistent data to identify trends and growth in the student learning process. The information provided by the automated system may allow aggregation at the classroom, school, district, or state levels which may help teachers to make adjustments in their instruction, while administrators may use this information for data-based policy decision making (Williamson et al., 2010).

Cost

The cost of the CCSS assessments is a major concern. Because both consortia are developing computer-administered tests, all schools will ultimately provide computers, increase the internet connection bandwidth, and provide technical support to students who take the tests. Although both consortia are developing multiple forms of each assessment and broad assessment windows to reduce the demand of the quantity of computers by staggering the assessment within each grade and subject, the costs and efforts to provide enough computers and fast internet access will ultimately increase. As for computer-adapted tests, the speed of response will depend on (a) the time required for the computer to score the response, (b) the speed of connection between the terminal and the scoring server, and (c) the capability of the scoring server to meet all of the scoring demands at the same time (Williamson et al., 2010). Therefore, greater investment is needed to update the hardware and software in current school systems. Moreover, school districts have to pay the consortia a fee to use the tests. Students in certain grade levels will have to take the formative and summative tests several times in a year, suggesting that the total cost of administering CCSS assessments will be much more than the current budget for testing in each state.

Other than the costs, validity of the scores from the tests will need to be examined. Although the tests are being developed by reputable testing companies (e.g., Pearson, Educational Testing Service, and CTB/McGraw-Hill), psychometric properties of these tests remain to be determined until student scores become available. Internal consistency, item difficulty, comparisons between person ability and item difficulty, and the optimal number of latent profiles underlying the student scores remain to be examined with empirical data. For example, both consortia are planning to establish cut-off scores so that students in each grade can be placed into four levels where Level III is considered "meeting the standard." However, this decision may be arbitrary because most states are adopting the same four proficiency levels. Will the data support this categorization? We will have to wait until empirical data become available. Furthermore, classical models of test validity divide validity into content validity, criteria validity, and construct validity.

Messick (1995) challenged the classical models of test validity and viewed validity as a single unitary construct, emphasizing the meaning and interpretation of the scores and implications for unbiased and fair use of scores. Therefore, with consultation of content area educational professors, teachers, and school administrators, these companies may be able to develop items for CCSS assessments with content validity. However, it is the interpretation and the fair use of the scores that will determine the validity of the student responses to those testing items. Hopefully, the testing companies will be able to avoid poor-quality items and scoring errors (Strauss, 2013). As Gewertz (2012) noted, CCSS test results might be used improperly to make important decisions, such as high school graduation, teacher evaluation, and school accountability. These outcomes are uncertain at this moment.

As with any newly administered tests, there will be redirection and reconsiderations as a number of incidents and glitches are reported. Recent accounts (Cavanagh, 2015; Gewertz 2015a, 2015b; Ujifusa, 2015), after the administration of the test in the spring of 2015, report problems in test supervision and organization. Some states have threatened to abandon the test because of technical difficulties during test administration. Servers could not accommodate the massive number of students taking the tests, causing interruptions (Ujifusa, 2015).

Test monitoring systems were another problem. There were some reports of students taking pictures of the test and sharing items on social media. As a result, schools need to adapt and develop more effective test-monitoring systems. Test item sharing has resulted in the consortium developing a plan of action to monitor this type of activity. Parents have expressed concerns about the consortium's monitoring of student activity on social media. A PARCC spokesman, however, shared that taking images of the test is the same as photocopying and it threatens test security (Cavanagh, 2015; Gewertz, 2015b).

Although students finished exams before the given length of time, the test presently can take up to 9 hours to administer. Along with other difficulties reported, the consortium is now working to shorten the duration of test by combining end-of-the-year and performance tests (Gewertz, 2015a).

School Environmental Challenges and Solutions: Smoothing Rough Places

If school districts are going to use the student performance on the CCSS assessments for teacher evaluation and school accountability, teachers will spend a lot of instruction time testing the students and preparing them for the tests. Instead of teaching the students the required content knowledge and skills, teachers will feel pressured to teach the students how to get higher scores on the tests (teaching to the test). Moreover, because CCSS assessments will include both formative and summative tests administered at least two times a year with a combination of multiple-choice items and open-ended short-answer questions and essays, CCSS assessments will certainly take a longer time for students to complete. As a result, the administration of these assessments will cost students instruction time. Other concerns about the CCSS assessments include a possible loss of local autonomy, overload of assessments, teacher stress, unresponsiveness to individual student needs, and loss of intrinsic motivation to learn the subject matter (Sheldon & Biddle, 1998).

The use of computer-administered assessments will likely increase demands for technology training and professional development. Although both consortia promise to use a combination of computer-administered and paper-and-pencil assessment in the first two years, schools will move to completely computer-administered assessments later. Schools will have to provide additional professional development to teachers about how to use technology (e.g., desktop computers, laptops, tablet PCs) and how to solve technical problems during the administration of the assessments, especially for teachers with technology phobia (Drew, 2013). As for scoring student responses to items in literacy assessments, automated scoring will score grammar, word use, mechanics, spelling, vocabulary, semantic content of essays, relevance to the prompt, and aspects of organization and flow. However, it cannot assess rhetorical voice, the logic of an argument, the extent to which a particular concept is accurately described, or whether specific ideas are well grounded. These holistic judgments must still come from human graders.

Although both consortia claim to include students with learning disabilities and students who are English language learners (ELLs, discussed further in Chapter 5), Kentucky is mentioned as deliberately focused on reaching high school dropouts and ensuring higher education and career readiness programs for all students (Jones & McGuinness, 2011). To reach the goals of CCSS, assessments have to be broadly accepted and consistently applied. With sound leadership and commitment of stakeholders, states may be able to use the assessments to ensure appropriate implementation of the CCSS initiative.

School-Based Leaders

Leaders will need to assist in the development of in-class formative assessments for day-to-day use. It is imperative that schools balance all data—quantitative and qualitative, formal and informal. Informal qualitative data should include not just the informal PARCC and SBAC assessments that are being fashioned, but checklist, artifacts, photographs, videos, parent feedback, etc. (Bellanca, Fogarty, Pete, & Stinson, 2013).

School-based leaders will need to do the following:

- Develop a schoolwide plan for assessment, monitoring systems, and communication of the scores to parents.
- Assist teachers in linking assessment to instruction.
- Devise tools to observe teaching and assessments (see Figure 3.1).
- Adapt formative assessments from multiple and varied data sources.

- Pilot test measures and then define problems (i.e., What is not working? What does quantitative and qualitative data tell us?).

- Examine issues, outcomes, strategies, and behavior and define benchmarks.

- Locate effective strategies to alleviate the mismatches and gaps in achievement, instruction, and assessment, set new innovative goals, and develop achievable criteria.

Special Education Leaders

Special education leaders should provide support for ongoing data collection within the Multi-tiered Systems of Support and Response to Intervention. These systems allow for the individual assessment and the instructional needs of students with disabilities and at-risk students. Again, collecting data and using it to make instructional decisions are paramount (McAssey, 2014)

Special education leaders will also need to focus on test accommodations and modifications for students with disabilities. Maxwell and Samuels (2013) grouped accommodations into two kinds: presentation accommodations and response accommodations. Presentation accommodations include varied materials, multiple technologies, or the format of materials that students with disabilities may need to access, for example, Braille or American Sign Language. Response accommodations allow students to reply to the test with adjustment, such as testing at a particular time of day or allowing the student to have frequent breaks. PARCC and SBAC have proposed some of these accommodations, for example, read-aloud software, the use of calculators, word-prediction software, American Sign Language videos, word definitions, and dictation or transcription software. Accommodations also include embedded Universal Design for Learning (UDL) tools that will allow students to highlight or enlarge certain words and sections of the test (Heitin, 2014).

Special education leaders will need to:

- make sure that general and special education teachers and leaders understand these features and have sufficient training to use them; and

- advocate that all communities, no matter the socioeconomic status, receive these features and software on their computers.

Applying the Common Core Standards and Solutions

School leaders will need to introduce CCSS formative assessment into the existing culture while encouraging and supporting teachers to design and refine classroom-based formative assessments. It is best if leaders move at a steady pace to create the assessments at each grade level and redesign as necessary. The following is important for leaders to remember (Ainsworth & Viegut, 2006).

The Common Core Teacher Observation Tool

KEY

Yes: *Behavior Observed*

No: *Behavior Not Observed* (notation suggested)

NI: *Behavior Needs Improvement* (notation required)

1	Demonstrates Professional Leadership	Yes	No	NI
a	Establishes and maintains positive interpersonal relationships with students, parents, and colleagues			
b	Establishes and maintains positive school-community relationships			
c	Shares knowledge and expertise about CCSS teaching and learning			
d	Shows initiative in developing educational policies and programs designed to improve student learning and well-being			
e	Functions as a productive team member			
f	Demonstrates commitment to school mission			

2	Demonstrates Content Knowledge	Yes	No	NI
a	Demonstrates competence in content knowledge within own discipline			
b	Accurately communicates the skills and core concepts related to certified academic areas			
c	Maintains current knowledge of discipline(s) taught			
d	Demonstrates content knowledge that allows for integration of ideas and information across the disciplines			
e	Connects content to real-world applications			
f	Presents content in a manner that reflects global perspective and sensitivity to individual differences and differentiation			

3	Designs Learning for All Students	Yes	No	NI
a	Designs instruction and formative assessment aligned with district and CCSS			
b	Designs clearly stated learning objectives that require students to think and process ideas at higher levels			
c	Designs lessons that connect content across disciplines			
d	Designs developmentally appropriate learning experiences that challenge, motivate, and actively involve the learner			
e	Develops and incorporates strategies that address individual needs (i.e., UDL, Inquiry Learning)			
f	Arranges physical environment of classroom to support student learning and behavior			
g	Includes appropriate use of available technology and other UDL experiences and differentiation in designing learning experiences for students			
h	Uses a variety of school and community resources to support learning			

Figure 3.1 CCSS teacher observation *(Continued)*

4 Demonstrates Effective Classroom Management	Yes	No	NI
a Develops rapport with individual students as a foundation for a successful classroom experience			
b Proactively teaches the behavior skills necessary for students to succeed in the classroom and school			
c Proactively teaches appropriate expectations for the different modes of classroom instruction			
d Establishes procedures that foster student responsibility and cooperation			
e Shows consistent sensitivity to individual differences			
f Demonstrates composure in managing student behavior			
g Handles student disciplinary incidents in accordance with school and district discipline plans and expectations			

5 Demonstrates Effective Teaching Practices	Yes	No	NI
a Establishes high expectations for students			
b Communicates specific learning objectives			
c Establishes and maintains positive rapport with students as a foundation for effective instruction			
d Connects learning with students' prior knowledge, experiences and backgrounds, and aspirations			
e Uses questioning and inquiry based strategies and/or written assignments that require students to develop and practice high-level thinking skills			
f Reinforces learning through explicit teaching, guided practice, independent practice, and homework aligned with classroom instruction			
g Closely monitors students' progress			
h Makes efficient use of physical and human resources and time			
i Models and/or demonstrates the skills, concepts, attributes, and/or thinking processes to be learned			
j Develops and uses multiple teaching/learning strategies that actively engage students			
k Uses available media and technology and UDL experiences to enhance classroom instruction			
l Provides opportunities for students to increase their knowledge of cultural diversity			
m Appropriately manages student examination of social issues relative to course content			
n Demonstrates competence in oral and written communication			

6 Assesses and Communicates Learning Results	Yes	No	NI
a Ensures that the program/department/district plans and activities are student centered			
b Utilizes data from the school community to meet student needs			
c Follows Board policy, laws, and regulations			
d Ensures that the environment in which schools operate is influenced on behalf of students and their families			
e Accurately and continuously uses and develops formative assessments to monitor student progress toward obtaining state and local goals			

		Yes	No	NI
f	Teaches students to self-assess			
g	Collects and analyzes assessment data from formative assessments, and SBAC and PARCC			
h	Maintains up-to-date records			
i	Communicates to students and parents expectations, criteria for assessment, and student strengths and weaknesses			
7	**Evaluates Teaching and Learning**	**Yes**	**No**	**NI**
a	Collects data and analyzes effectiveness of instruction			
b	Modifies instruction based on feedback, reflection, and assessment			
c	Assesses/evaluates effectiveness of programs, curricula, plans, and activities			
d	Based on reflections, makes recommendations for needed adjustments			
8	**Demonstrates Effective Collaboration**	**Yes**	**No**	**NI**
a	Collaborates to support student learning			
b	Collaborates with teachers in other disciplines to analyze and structure cross-disciplinary approaches to instruction			
c	Demonstrates productive team membership			
d	Actively participates in PLCs and other instructional teams			
e	Contacts parents to discuss social and academic progress of students			
f	Recognizes and responds appropriately to differences in abilities, contributions, and social/cultural backgrounds			
g	Actively participates in RTI and MTSS grade-level meetings			
9	**Demonstrates Professional Growth**	**Yes**	**No**	**NI**
a	Identifies professional growth objectives and activities which relate to the vision and mission of the school			
b	Analyzes student performance to help identify PD needs			
c	Prioritizes professional growth needs			
d	Applies to instruction the knowledge, skills, and processes acquired through professional development			
e	Self-assesses impact of professional development activities			
10	**Demonstrates integration of technology and other UDL experiences**	**Yes**	**No**	**NI**
a.	Utilizes a variety of multi-media tools and UDL to enhance productivity and support student learning			
b	Requests and uses appropriate assistive and adaptive devices for students with special needs			
c	Designs lessons that use available technology and other UDL experiences to address diverse student needs and learning styles			
d	Instructs and supervises students in ethical and legal use of technology			
11	**Carries Out Professional Responsibilities**	**Yes**	**No**	**NI**
a	Is punctual			
b	Completes and maintains accurate records			

Figure 3.1 (Continued)

c	Completes job requirements according to timelines
d	Adheres to requirements of the school employee handbook, district policies, and state statutes and regulations
e	Carries out responsibilities according to job description
f	Complies with the code of ethics for teachers
g	Demonstrates competence in written and verbal communication
h	Discusses student and school issues in a professional manner with students, parents, and colleagues

Notations and Suggestions
Designed by Mickey Dunaway

Figure 3.1 (Continued)

- Begin to design formative measures with teachers at the various grade levels who have a desire to develop the CCSS pilot formative, in-class assessments. Professionals who have knowledge of ELLs and students with disabilities should be on the team. The designed assessments should match instruction and align with the anchor standards.

- Assessment should be aligned with PARCC and SBAC formal assessment and collaboratively scored by grade-level teams or Professional Learning Communities (PLCs).

- Assessments should be piloted on students to help determine validity. The assessments can be redesigned according to the findings and outcomes of the tests, examining specific items which need to be aligned to CCSS.

School and special education leaders will need to determine if the assessments (Ainsworth & Viegut, 2006)

- are varied enough to measure proficiency levels of all students, including ELLs;
- can be used with UDL or other methods that differentiate instruction;
- are adaptable to multiple measures; and
- have a range of testing high or low thinking and problem-solving skills.

Collaborative scoring guides or rubric criteria, a scoring system, and methods for interrater reliability can be developed by PLCs for the assessment items.

Connections to Assessment

Formal quantitative assessments measure differences among groups, while formative, in-class assessments focus on individual students and have an impact on the child's academic growth. Summative, formal assessments provide information for broad curricular changes, while formative, informal assessments lead to better instruction. Both are important because assessments if used in isolation, without the countermeasures, do not give an accurate assessment of a child. Formal measures coupled with informal measures provide a more complete picture of students' strengths and challenges, and leaders and teachers need both to improve instruction and student learning.

Research-Based Practical Tips and Caveats

- Formal and informal, quantitative and qualitative, formative and summative measures are all needed in school districts and schools to obtain a clearer picture of a student performance.

- PARCC and SBAC are formulating formative assessments; however, each school and district may tailor its own according to the student characteristics in a district. PLCs can help develop, pilot, test, and redesign these formative, in-class assessments.

- Special education leaders will need to monitor the accommodations and modifications provided for students with disabilities to ensure fairness of test administrations.

- Teachers will need training with test administration of PARCC and SBAC and developing formative assessments.

- Leaders should make sure that all types of data are used:

  - Academic—subjects and subject areas by teacher and grade, and school-wide data on measured standards in areas such as reading or math, grade distributions across demographic groups from report cards.

  - Formal—because of the length of time between instruction and assessments, these are typically summative by quarter and year.

  - Formative—primarily classroom-based assessments including common assessments from PLCs which provide information for revising instructional methods to achieve mastery during the current unit of study.

  - Environmental—culture, climate, and schoolwide processes that affect performance.

  - Demographic—external cultural factors.

- Leaders should:

  - put the data in a user-friendly format—tables and charts are best;

  - present it in small chunks—this prevents data fatigue;

  - trust the teachers to analyze it—that way they will own the data;

  - use it (all of it, not just the scores)—build an improvement plan; and

  - build a data plan—to determine if the improvement plan is working.

Summary

This chapter provided information about the two main CCSS-connected assessments, PARCC and SBAC, but the expertise of PLCs, teacher leaders, and other leadership staff is also critical to help design and pilot in-class assessments and to use the data provided by all formative and summative assessments to assist in instruction. However, leaders will need to carefully guide the staff with the administration, recognizing that the staff has had little course work or professional development on the processes of testing and measurement. Therefore, learning a new vocabulary of assessment is critical. The concepts need not be statistics-filled. Most key assessment concepts like reliability and validity are easily understood. As teachers become more knowledgeable in the area of assessment best practices, principals should also begin to see improvement in classroom-based assessments as well. As we began this chapter, we were eavesdropping on a conversation about data between Assistant Principal Driven and Principal Collection. As we read in this chapter, all data need to be analyzed, both quantitative and qualitative, to get a true picture of the school and the students therein.

The PARCC and the SBAC both provide formal summative data to measure student progress over the year's instruction. Likely this is not all the data that Mrs. Driven is analyzing—at least it should not be. There are multiple forms of data that should be considered when looking at the performance of a school and before developing strategies to improve that performance.

References

Ainsworth, L., & Viegut, D. (2006). *Common formative assessments: How to connect standards based assessments*. Thousand Oaks, CA: Corwin Press.

Anderson, L. W., & Krathwohl, D. R. (Eds.). (2001). *A taxonomy for learning, teaching and assessing: A revision of Bloom's Taxonomy of educational objectives*. New York, NY: Longman.

Bellanca, J. A., Fogarty, R. J., & Pete, B. M. (2012). *How to teach thinking skills within the Common Core: 7 key student proficiencies of the new national standards*. Bloomington, IN: Solution Tree Press.

Bellanca, J. A., Fogarty, R. J., Pete, B. M., & Stinson, R. L. (2013). *School leader's guide to the Common Core: Achieving results through rigor and relevance*. Bloomington, IN: Solution Tree.

Bloom, B. S., & Krathwohl, D. R. (1956). *Taxonomy of educational objectives: The classification of educational goals, by a committee of college and university examiners. Handbook 1: Cognitive domain*. New York, NY: Longmans.

Cavanagh, S. (2015, March 25). Pearson, PARCC knocked for monitoring students' social media. *Education Week, 34*, 25.

Drew, S. (2013). Open up the ceiling on the Common Core State Standards: Preparing students for 21st-century literacy—Now. *Journal of Adolescent & Adult Literacy, 56*(4), 321–330.

Gewertz, C. (2012, September 19). Will the Common Core assessments be used as a graduation requirement? *Education Week*. Retrieved from http://blogs.edweek.org/edweek/curriculum/2012/09/common_core_tests_to_replace.html

Gewertz, C. (2015a, May 13). Students snap pictures of PARCC test, teachers disciplined. *Education Week, 34*, 30.

Gewertz, C. (2015b, April 22). PARCC consortium working to shorten test time. *Education Week, 34*, 28.

Heitin, L. (2014). Testing plans differ on accommodations. *Education Week, 33*(29), 530–533.

Jones, D., & McGuinness, A. C. (2011). State capacity for leadership: Ensuring meaningful higher education involvement in state implementation of new assessments aligned with the Common Core State Standards. *National Center for Higher Education Management Systems.* Retrieved from http://www.nchems.org

Lane, S. (2010). *Performance assessment: The state of the art* (SCOPE Student Performance Assessment Series). Stanford, CA: Stanford Center for Opportunity Policy in Education.

Maxwell, L., & Samuels, C. A. (2013). PARCC proposes Common-Core test accommodations. *Education Week, 32*(29), 6.

McAssey, L. (2014). Common Core assessments: A principal's view. *Principal, 93*(3), 14–19. Retrieved from http://www.naesp.org

Messick, S. (1995). Validity of psychological assessment: Validation of inferences from persons' responses and performances as scientific inquiry into score meaning. *American Psychologist, 50*(9), 741–749.

Porter-Magee, K., O'Leary, J. D., & Partin, E. (2011). *The Common Core and the future of student assessment in Ohio.* Retrieved from http://files.eric.ed.gov/fulltext/ED524355.pdf

Sheldon, K. M., & Biddle, B. J. (1998). Standards, accountability, and school reform: Perils and pitfalls. *Teachers College Record, 100*(1), 164–180.

Smarter Balanced Assessment Consortium. (2014). *Smarter balanced states approve achievement level recommendations.* Retrieved from http://www.edweek.org/media/achievement-levels-and-scale-scores-final.pdf

Strauss, V. (2013). *A brief history of Pearson's problems with testing.* Retrieved from http://www.washingtonpost.com/blogs/answer-sheet/wp/2013/04/24/a-brief-history-of-pearsons-problems-with-testing/

Ujifusa, A. (2015, April 22). Glitches plague testing online in three states. *Education Week, 34*, 28.

Willhoft, J. L. (2012). Next-generation assessments aligned to the Common Core. *School Administrator, 11*(69), 30–33.

Williamson, D. M., Bennett, R. E., Lazer, S., Bernstein, J., Foltz, P. W., Landauer, T. K., . . . Sweeney, K. (2010). *Automated scoring for the assessment of Common Core Standards.* Retrieved from https://www.ets.org/s/commonassessments/pdf/AutomatedScoringAssessCommon-CoreStandards.pdf

Zimmerman, B. J. (2000). Attaining self-regulation: A social cognitive perspective. In M. Boekaerts, P. R. Pintrich, & M. Zeidner (Eds.), *Handbook of self-regulation* (pp. 13–39). San Diego, CA: Academic Press.

CHAPTER

Young Children and Their Families

Vivian I. Correa, Ya-yu Lo, and Dawson R. Hancock

Katie, a six-year-old girl with a traumatic brain injury, attends a mixed kindergarten and first-grade classroom in a rural farm community with a population of approximately 1,000 residents. She lives with her grandparents, parents, and an older brother, aged 14, on their 50-acre family-owned farm. They are struggling to make ends meet because of the growing costs of agricultural chemicals, genetically modified seeds, farm equipment, and technology. The family owns some livestock, including Katie's horse, but is solely dependent on their corn and cotton crops. Katie receives direct special education services once a week for two hours for moderate learning impairments in language, memory, and attention from an itinerant special education teacher who travels 50 miles each way to the school. Katie's mother wants the teachers to provide her with more intensive academic instruction. Although Katie's general education teacher, Ms. Ogle, is accepting of Katie's inclusion in the classroom, she does not have much background in special education, is under school district pressure to use the Common Core standards to improve her students' achievement scores, and is challenged by the lack of school resources associated with high poverty in the district. The principal has asked that all teachers attend a 3-day professional development workshop on the CCSS scheduled during the summer in the adjoining town 50 miles away. How do we address the increasing pressures Ms. Ogle feels about teaching the Common Core standards to her students while also supporting Katie's special education needs and involving her family in her education?

Introduction

The CCSS initiative has been "one of the most ambitious attempts to overhaul education policy in the country's history" (Cavanagh, 2012, p. 14). The instructional shift to national standards has significantly affected how and what students will be taught across K–12 education. For example, a change in English language arts is to provide students additional chances to read nonfiction texts (i.e., biographies, autobiographies). A change in mathematics is to demonstrate to students how math works and ask students to discuss their understanding (DeLorenzo, 2014).

The shift has affected administrators, teachers, children, parents, and caregivers in countless ways; the impact it has had on assessment, curriculum, and instruction of kindergarten and primary grade children has been significant. Furthermore, the impact the CCSS will have on the education of young children, including those with disabilities, continues to be an area of concern (Main, 2012). *Meeting the needs of young children with disabilities* requires educational leaders to become advocates for an inclusive system of education centered on all children and families. The vignette illustrates the challenges teachers and families of children with disabilities face when resources are limited but the school's expectations to implement the CCSS are high. This chapter will include discussion on how instructional leaders and early childhood teachers[1] can support the implementation of the CCSS for young children in grades K–3 and how families can be involved in the implementation of the standards at home and in school.

Are CCSS for Young Children Too Much and Too Soon?

Many professionals decry the CCSS movement stating that the heavily academic-based orientation of the standards diminishes the role of developmentally appropriate and play-oriented practices embraced by early childhood teachers (Gallant, 2009; Graue, 2009; Main, 2012; Pretti-Frontczak, 2014). Although the pressures to focus on young children's reading and mathematics skills have increased over the past 20 years, the CCSS have dramatically changed the way kindergarten educators are teaching in the classroom (Gallant, 2009). Specifically, teachers are under pressure to have children perform well on high-stakes assessments linked to the standards. The result of the CCSS movement has created a shift in curriculum and instructional practices that more closely align to the standards (Zwiers, O'Hara, & Pritchard, 2014). The focus on language arts at the K–3 level includes reading, writing, speaking, and listening across all subjects, including science, history, social studies, and arts. The focus on mathematics at the K–3 level includes addition/subtraction, multiplication/division, fractions, time, money, and solving problems using math concepts.

For some early childhood teachers, the increased focus on academics leaves them with little autonomy and flexibility in making curricular decisions based on developmentally appropriate practices (Gallant, 2009). Kindergarten teachers, in particular, worry that children are being asked to spend more time at their seats on academic skills and less time on motor activities, dramatic play, and learning centers (Gallant, 2009; Main, 2012). Further, the standards do not address benchmarks related to social and emotional development and approaches to learning (NAEYC & NAECS-SDE, 2010). Social, communication, and self-regulation skills are as critical for young children's learning in the early years as naming upper- and lower-case letters, matching those letters with their sounds, and printing them. Teachers also worry that some young students will enter kindergarten not ready for the academic tasks and experience failure at an early age with possible referrals to special education and/or support services (Gallant, 2009). Additionally, it is likely that parents will be expected to increase their involvement in teaching higher level literacy and mathematics skills outside of school.

On the other hand, other early childhood professionals believe the adoption of the CCSS is not a detriment to K–3 young children if teachers are effectively prepared to transform their instructional practices by participating in intensive and long-term professional development activities targeted at classroom strategies that align with the CCSS (Kramer-Vida, Levitt, & Kelly, 2012). Kramer-Vida et al. (2012) found that after a year of intensive professional development on using writing workshops, kindergarten teachers got their students to not only meet the CCSS writing standards but also exceed them. To prepare K–3 teachers for the transformation, school leaders must provide:

- time during the school day;
- paid classroom substitutes to help teachers concentrate on the work; and
- literacy and mathematics coaches to assist in modeling classroom practices and assist teachers through the transformational change process.

While the standards have promise for all students, concerns remain about how to achieve the high expectations for younger students, students with disabilities, and students from diverse or at-risk backgrounds. The child in the vignette, Katie, exemplifies a population of students who may struggle to meet the standards. The work of educating Katie will be challenging and will require the support of administrators, teachers, therapists, community leaders, and family members. A team effort will be required to implement an educational program that meets her needs, adequately evaluates her gains on reliable and valid outcome measures, and involves her family in an authentic and meaningful way.

Family Involvement in CCSS Initiatives

Over the past several years, supporters of the Common Core standards have included elected officials, academic scholars, and school personnel. The need to include families in the discussion of the CCSS has become an important part of school district planning (Cavanagh, 2012; Neuman & Roskos, 2013; Nick, 2014). The CCSS documents are lengthy and technical and parents may be concerned about how they will affect their child's education (Elish-Piper, 2013). Several national organizations (e.g., National Parent Teacher Association [National PTA], National Council of La Raza) and prominent leaders (e.g., the Bill & Melinda Gates Foundation) have supported parent outreach initiatives by developing written and online materials, videos, and public service announcements on the CCSS (Cavanagh, 2012). For example, the National PTA's goal is for parents to be knowledgeable about the standards and new assessments and to support them as states implement the standards (National PTA, n.d.). However, tailoring the message to address families at the local level is critical for the success of the Common Core initiative. Families need more than a brochure to inform them about the CCSS. They need to understand what the standards mean and what they need to do at home to promote their child's success in school. The information must be delivered in multiple formats and languages to meet the needs of all families, including those from diverse ethnic, cultural, socioeconomic, and geographic backgrounds. Family involvement in the CCSS can be done at multiple levels, including (a) individual parent–teacher level, (b) classroom level, (c) school-building level, and (d) district and community level.

Individual Parent–Teacher Level

For parents of five- or six-year-olds, understanding that the goals of the CCSS are to make their child ready for success in college and the workforce can be confusing. Teachers and administrators need to help parents understand how they can start as early as kindergarten to help their children become "college- and career-ready" by building foundations for core academic content knowledge.

For parents of children with disabilities like Katie, teachers need to be extra diligent in explaining how the CCSS may affect the development and implementation of the individualized education programs (IEPs), as well as their child's performance in the classroom. Parents may be overly concerned that their child is already struggling with academics, and the standards will further increase the expectations of their child for academic performance. Parents may want to know how the special education team will support their child in understanding the standards, how the standards will be reflected in the child's IEP, and how they will assess the child's progress toward meeting their grade-level standards. Parents need to be assured that their child's teachers are knowledgeable about the new standards and are prepared to individualize instruction with evidence-based teaching strategies (https://www.engageny.org/). Leaders should assure that:

- General and special education teachers provide multiple opportunities for parents to meet with them about the CCSS and the teachers' answer inquiries about the expectations for children with disabilities to meet grade-level standards.
- Accommodations and modifications needed to address the standards-based curriculum are provided.
- Meetings should occur in multiple settings, including the home, the community, and the school.
- Visits to the home provide important information on the families' strengths, needs, and resources.
- Teachers integrate educational activities into the families' life routines.

In Katie's case, it would be important for leaders to assure that:

- Teachers understand the connections that can be made with her life on the farm and the standards-based curriculum.
- Katie's family is provided individualized activities that can be done at home to support Katie's progress in language arts and mathematics (i.e., Katie can be involved in helping her parents count the number of animals on the family's farm to keep track of their whereabouts).
- Teachers should regularly report to the parents on Katie's progress toward meeting her IEP goals and the state standards.
- Katie's family is provided with samples of her work and ways to support activities at home and in the community.

Families play an important role in supporting CCSS at home, and they should be encouraged to ask about what their child is learning at school, review and discuss homework, communicate regularly with their child's teachers, attend school events to learn about teachers' expectations, and attend public meetings to learn about the standards (https://www.engageny.org/). An example of a kindergarten roadmap developed by the Council of the Greater City Schools is provided on this website—www.cgcs.org. It provides families with guidance on what their children will be learning in English language arts and how they can support that learning in kindergarten as well as provides a 3-year snapshot showing how selected standards progress in grades 1 and 2.

Leaders and the Classroom Level

Leaders can assure that families are provided with information on the CCSS through various forms of communication. There are many ways to involve and educate parents at the classroom level (https://www.engageny.org/):

- Newsletters, e-mails, and access to a classroom website (Cavanagh, 2012)
- Multiple languages and be jargon-free
- Open house events to communicate with parents
- Examples of classroom activities
- Handouts and brochures
- Partnering with parent volunteers when planning and organizing the open house events
- Invitation to parents to visit the classroom to see how lessons are delivered in support of their children's learning that aligns with CCSS

Leaders and the School Level

At the school level, administrators, teachers, and community leaders can reach out to parents in multiple ways. School leaders can do the following:

- Use the school advisory council or the PTA to assist in organizing schoolwide workshops and activities related to CCSS.
- Partner with local universities to host workshops or provide information on evidence-based practices for implementing CCSS with special student populations such as English language learners (ELLs) and students with disabilities (Nick, 2014).
- Assess formats that will be most effective for engaging with parents (e.g., lectures, round table discussions, town hall meetings).
- Provide national and state organizations' websites and materials for parent education on CCSS (e.g., www.pta.org).
- Offer parent guides that include:
  (a) key items children should be learning in English language arts and mathematics in each grade, and
  (b) methods for helping parents build stronger relationships with their child's teacher.

The Council of the Great City Schools (www.cgcs.org) has provided parent roadmaps to the CCSS on their website. The roadmaps, available in both English and Spanish, provide guidance to parents about what their children will be learning in language arts and mathematics and how they can support that learning in grades K–8. New York State Education Department provides a series of toolkits with materials for planning parent workshops on the CCSS (https://www.engageny.org/). The website offers planning tools for parent night sessions and parent handouts that can be downloaded in Word document format and customized with an e-mail address and contact information. These resources are valuable to educators in reaching out to families about the CCSS and in helping them to understand their roles in supporting their child's learning and meeting the standards. Administrators should use multiple methods to notify parents of the CCSS initiatives, by sending the notice home with students, posting it on the school website, and announcing it via social media. Table 4.1 provides a list of resources that can be provided to parents at the school level.

Leaders and the District and Community Level

State and local school districts can also be valuable sources of information on the CCSS for parents. The Center for Parent Information and Resources (http://www.parentcenterhub.org/) provides information organized topically for administrators,

Table 4.1 CCSS Resources for Families

Resource	URL	Description
A Parent's Guide to the Common Core Standards	http://www.education.com/magazine/article/parents-guide-to-common-core-standards/	The webpage provides parents with tips on how they can support the CCSS at home
Center for Parent Information and Resources	http://www.parentcenterhub.org/repository/commoncore/	The website provides a variety of parent resources in English and Spanish on CCSS and students with disabilities
Colorín Colorado	http://www.colorincolorado.org/common-core/parents/faq/	The website provides 10 things parents should know about the CCSS
Council of the Great City Schools: Common Core Works	http://www.commoncoreworks.org/site/default.aspx?PageID=239	The 3-minute video, available in Spanish and English, explains how the CCSS will help children achieve at high levels and get ready for graduation and beyond
Council of the Great City Schools: Parent Roadmaps	http://www.cgcs.org/Domain/36	The website offers roadmaps that provide parents guidance on what their children will be learning in English language arts and how they can support that learning in grades K–8. The roadmaps also provide 3-year snapshots showing how selected standards progress from year to year
Engage NY Toolkit for Parent Engagement	https://www.engageny.org/resource/planning-a-parent-workshop-toolkit-for-parent-engagement	The toolkit provides training materials for parents including planning tools, documents, and agendas to help prepare for and deliver a parent workshop on CCSS
PTA Parent Guides	http://www.pta.org/parents/content.cfm?ItemNumber=2583	The guides were developed by teachers, parents, and administrators to provide key items that children should be learning in English language arts and mathematics in each grade and activities that parents can do at home to help their children learn
Teaching Channel	https://www.teachingchannel.org/videos/common-core-standards-ela	This video series offers a more detailed introduction to the standards and what they might look like in the classroom

educators, and families on the CCSS. For families, there is information on what is happening in each state and how the standards apply to children with disabilities. Leaders can:

- host town hall meetings with district-level personnel and provide community-wide workshops on policies and implementation of the CCSS; and

- involve state education agencies to support community outreach efforts by providing updates on policies and procedures related to CCSS on their website.

Young Children At Risk and with Disabilities

Early childhood teachers are being challenged to meet the early literacy and mathematics needs of young children at risk for learning difficulties while trying to maintain classroom discipline and attend to the social and emotional needs of the children. A large number of children enter school not ready to learn due to social and environmental risk factors. For example, young children who live in poverty in urban or rural areas, who are from a non-English language background, who have a single or teen mother who has low education levels, or who have no access to high-quality child care are at risk for school failure (Robbins, Stagman, & Smith, 2012). Many of these children are struggling to meet the CCSS for kindergarten, and early childhood teachers are often frustrated with how to accommodate their educational needs in the classroom (Gallant, 2009).

Kindergarten standards require students to be able to produce the sounds for letters, read common high-frequency words, and read emergent reader texts with purpose and understanding. Kent, Wanzek, and Al Otaiba (2012) found that kindergarten students at risk for reading difficulties spent very little time during the scheduled reading instructional block participating in literacy activities, such as text reading, comprehension, vocabulary, fluency, or spelling. What was most alarming was that students were actively engaged in reading print for approximately one minute per instructional session. Most of their time was spent in choral reading with few opportunities for feedback from their teachers. Without systemic and intentional instruction that will produce active engagement in academic learning and responding, at-risk young children are unlikely to meet the Common Core standards.

Young children with identified disabilities further experience higher level of challenges to master grade-level standards. As described in the opening vignette, assuring that Katie makes progress toward achieving grade-level mastery may be challenging for her parents, teachers, and administrators. Although she will continue to be served in her general education classroom, she will need specially designed instruction (i.e., special education, related services, assistive technology, supplemental aids, accommodations, and/or modifications) to achieve the kindergarten standards. Young children with disabilities may have a difficult time with accessing the CCSS at grade level because they lack the primary skills to process at higher cognitive levels (Morgan et al., 2014).

School Environment Challenges: Smoothing Rough Places

In order to support young children at risk or with disabilities, general and special education leaders need to analyze the components and requirements of the CCSS and assure that instruction will attend to these children's needs. According to Morgan et al. (2014), the creation of a task analysis for a specific grade-level standard provides teachers with the list of skills and the order in which they need to be learned. The process of unwrapping the academic content standards provides teachers with a deep understanding of the instructional objectives that need to be taught and the mastery assessments needed to track student progress (Morgan et al., 2014). For example, the North Carolina Department of Public Instruction unpacked the CCSS to support educators in learning what the standards mean for a child to know, to understand, and to be able to do. General and special education leaders must collaborate so that special education teachers can then use the resources for unpacked content of the CCSS to work with general education teachers in designing instruction using evidence-based practices within a multi-tiered system of support to address the unique needs of students with disabilities.

Multi-tiered Systems of Support for Achieving CCSS Learning

In order to achieve grade-level CCSS, young children at risk for academic underachievement and those with disabilities are in need of evidence-based instructional strategies much more so than their peers without disabilities. Substantial research has suggested that early interventions with an explicit, highly structured, and carefully sequenced curriculum can reduce the number of children being identified at risk for future academic failure (Kamps et al., 2008). Early intervention efforts in academics for children at risk for developing a disability have centered on the prevention of reading and mathematics difficulties in early grades, as early as kindergarten, through highly intensive and systematic instruction with a multi-tiered system of support that offers varying levels of intensity in instruction (Doabler et al., 2014; Kamps et al., 2008). A multi-tiered system of support is an evidence-based model of education that uses a systematic data-based problem-solving approach to provide academic and/or behavioral interventions according to children's varying needs (Problem Solving & Response to Intervention Project, Florida's Positive Behavior Support Project, & University of South Florida, 2011). According to Gamm et al. (2012), a multi-tiered system of supports provides a framework for teachers to determine "how and when" to teach skills identified in CCSS so that early intervention and differentiated instruction can be provided to support children who are not on track academically before they develop persistent and significant academic failure. Specifically, the tiered model of prevention and interventions allows teachers to intensify instruction based on the responsiveness of children who may have increasing academic needs through three tiers of supports (Fuchs & Vaughn, 2012). A well-designed core curriculum (reading or mathematics) at the primary tier of support offers the foundation for *all* children's early academic learning where they are exposed to clear teacher modeling of new concepts (e.g., number sense, letter-sound identification) and receive ample opportunities for guided and independent practice with performance feedback (Doabler, Fien, Nelson-Walker, & Baker, 2012). The secondary level of support provides at-risk children with supplemental academic instruction in small group, in addition to the core program, to remediate academic difficulties. At the tertiary level, children who are unresponsive to primary and secondary levels of support receive additional pull-out instruction that aims at intensifying skills-based supports with multiple opportunities to practice, monitored feedback, and progress monitoring (Gamm et al., 2012).

Research has identified explicit instructional design principles as a defining feature of effective interventions within the multi-tiered systems of support (Doabler et al., 2014; Kamps et al., 2008; Spencer, Goldstein, & Kaminski, 2012). Explicit instruction is a systematic and structured instructional approach that has an intentional design and delivery of information, as well as a strong focus on learning for mastery through clearly defined teacher modeling and guidance and students' practice with error correction (Carnine, Silbert, Kame'enui, & Tarver, 2004). The principles of explicit instruction, including teaching for depth of understanding, repeated exposure to active responding and practice opportunities, and performance feedback, provide the structure necessary for promoting success of young children at risk or with disabilities in achieving CCSS learning. For example, Clarke et al. (2011) found that a yearlong, core mathematics curriculum that embeds explicit instruction and focuses on the CCSS for mathematics at the kindergarten level produced significant gains in mathematics achievement of at-risk students when compared to the achievement of at-risk peers in the comparison classrooms. Bryant et al. (2008) and Kamps et al. (2008) also demonstrated that secondary and tertiary levels of support with embedded explicit instruction, delivered in small group settings, improved the mathematics and reading achievement of at-risk kindergarten and first-grade students, respectively.

Applying the multi-tiered systems of support to Katie and other at-risk students in the school to promote the CCSS content learning, Ms. Ogle, Katie's general education teacher, will need to deliver an evidence-based core program in reading and mathematics with high fidelity to all kindergarten students in her general education classroom to build fundamental skills addressed in CCSS.

In regard to Katie's mother's concern about academic progress, Ms. Ogle can further involve Katie's family by:

- supporting Katie by practicing the same skills taught at school to build fluency and generalization at home; and

- getting additional small-group or individualized instruction with explicit instructional design principles on reading and mathematics contents.

Based on progress monitoring scores of the students' learning (e.g., assessing the number of letters and sounds a student can correctly identify in one minute), students with limited progress students like Katie can receive what they need. The high expectations set by the CCSS make it even more important for under-achieving students and those with disabilities to access high-quality instruction. Multi-tiered systems of support that embed explicit instructional design principles and evidence-based strategies offer teachers with tools for delivering high-quality instruction with varying duration and intensities that can prepare students with diverse instructional needs in meeting or exceeding the CCSS (Gamm et al., 2012).

School Leaders

The implementation of the CCSS in today's schools has challenged school leaders, teachers, and parents to make sure that all children are successful in reaching the goals of being college- and career-ready, particularly for young children and those with disabilities. School leaders are being charged with implementing and aligning the CCSS with curriculum and assessment practices. They are responsible for preparing teachers for the shift to standards-based instruction and assessment and informing parents about how this shift affects their children's education. For educators of children with disabilities, this includes adequately developing and implementing standards-based IEPs, with annual goals and short-term objectives aligned with grade-level standards (such as the CCSS). School leaders must also pay careful attention to the balance between academics, developmentally appropriate instruction, and social development for K–2 young children with and without disabilities. The skills developed in the early primary years are the most critical in predicting school success in the later years (Duncan et al., 2007). School leaders must create a school culture that supports change, open communication, and shared decision making when addressing the work associated with implementing the CCSS (Willhoft, 2012). It will be important to build teams of teachers, parents, and community leaders to support the CCSS efforts and to ensure that resources are provided for successful implementation of standards-based education.

Special Education Leaders

Ensuring that young children with disabilities are successful in meeting their grade-level standards will be largely dependent on a strong special education leader. Standards-based IEPs have received increased attention in recent years, particularly for those with severe disabilities (Courtade, Spooner, Browder, & Jimenez, 2012; Lynch & Adams, 2008). Special education teachers and related service personnel will need the support of building-level leaders and special education leaders to be successful in implementing standards-based IEPs and the CCSS with their students. Special education leaders can support the standards-based reform efforts by providing extensive professional development activities for their staff on the CCSS and how to align students' IEP goals and objectives to the grade-level standards. Support from the school leaders to facilitate successful collaboration between special and general education teachers in order to develop and implement standards-based IEPs will also be crucial.

To enhance the successful adoption of CCSS with young children in schools, several practices must be in place. These include professional development, promoting the use of instructional resources and technology, and preparation of school leadership.

Applying the Common Core Standards and Solutions

All states that have adopted the CCSS have reported statewide and local professional development initiatives to help teachers implement the standards, revise curriculum materials, and implement new assessments (Kober & Rentner, 2012). Both special and general education leaders must ensure that:

- Professional development for K–2 teachers be focused on evidence-based practices that capitalize on young children's desire for learning through exploration, play, and social interaction while addressing the language arts and mathematics standards (Gallant, 2009).

- Instructional practices for the early primary grades fall into a separate category than those for the upper grades.

- The professional development needs of their K–2 teachers be specific to the K–2 age range.

- Communities of practice be an effective structure for assuring that teachers and school staff engage in ongoing teacher learning, teamwork, and planning (Cashman, Linehan, & Rosser, 2007).

- Support to teachers be provided for teamwork and planning by adding additional staff to their classrooms such as paraprofessionals, volunteers, and college/university interns.

- Several CCSS training materials such as online modules, webinars, and web-streaming of television broadcasts be provided to school staff for professional development (Anderson, Harrison, & Lewis, 2012).

There are several sites that provide suggestions:

1   The James B. Hunt, Jr. Institute for Educational Leadership and Policy has produced a series of 54 short videos that introduce the CCSS and cover topics such as implications of using the standards with ELLs, reflections from school leaders on the changes CCSS have made in their schools, and information on the CCSS in Spanish (http://www.youtube.com/user/TheHuntInstitute).

2   Student Achievement Partners (www. achievethecore.org) have developed a variety of free professional development modules to help teachers implement the CCSS. They have iTunes U courses designed for different grade-level standards, so K–2 teachers can target their professional development by viewing courses on English and language arts for K–2 and mathematics for K–5.

3   The New York State Education Department provides school leaders and teachers a variety of resources and turnkey kits for implementing the CCSS in classrooms (https://www.engageny.org/resource/common-core-toolkit).

4   Materials on parent engagement, universal design for learning, and a complete turnkey series of eight sessions on strategies for adapting the curriculum to meet the needs of ELLs and students with disabilities.

Technology

Technology is key to preparing children to be college- and career-ready. It is also an important part of the supports that are necessary for instructional decision making (e.g., data collection) and implementation of instruction (Gamm et al., 2012). Technology also ensures that supports for children with special learning needs are individualized and portable. School leaders may find it challenging to find resources to support the technology needs of students and teachers at a time when school budgets are limited. Leaders may also not have the adequate infrastructure in their schools to support the CCSS online adaptive testing, the internet access and bandwidth, and the personnel expertise to address the technology issues that may arise during the test administration (Kober & Rentner, 2012). Partnership with school advisory councils, PTAs, and community leaders can provide opportunities to write grants and raise funds for targeted school initiatives such as purchasing iPads, laptops, and internet support for schools.

School leadership preparation programs must provide opportunities for future school and special education leaders to integrate the CCSS into the knowledge and skills needed for school administration and supervision (Houchens & Cabrera, 2013). Students in leadership preparation programs must be able to provide focused feedback on teaching practices based on the CCSS curricula and understand the importance of formative and summative assessments within classrooms and schools.

Connections to Assessment

Currently, standardized assessments are not being developed for K–2 students, but teachers are feeling the pressure to prepare children for third-grade testing. For example, kindergarten teachers in the Gallant (2009) study were frustrated that the pressure to teach more academics would require more "sit down" work and worksheets and less time for children to explore and play. Leaders can assist teachers with:

- Ongoing assessments that provide valuable information on the progress children are making toward the CCSS without sacrificing high-quality developmentally appropriate instruction.

- Designing formative assessments that provide teachers with a deep understanding of what the young children know and are able to do will be the challenge facing teachers, parents, and school leaders integrating the CCSS in instructional planning (Heitin, 2014).

- Defining progress-monitoring requirements and criteria for determining the need for students to receive intensified intervention at the secondary and tertiary levels.

- Practices that include curriculum-based assessments and ongoing progress monitoring to be integral to collecting data on individual children and adjusting lessons plans and interventions to improve individual achievement.

- Multi-tiered systems of support framework.

- Frequent and ongoing progress monitoring to determine "responsiveness" of students to instruction.

According to Gamm et al. (2012), progress monitoring data allow school staff to determine whether a student is making progress on certain CCSS skills at an adequate rate within a given time frame and whether the student is in need of more intensive instruction or intervention. The frequency (e.g., quarterly, monthly, weekly) and types of assessment (e.g., benchmark assessment, diagnostic assessment) may also vary based on the intensities of students' needs.

Children entering third grade will be assessed on one of two new computer-based assessments developed by Partnership for the Assessment of Readiness for College and Careers (PARCC, 2014) and the SMARTER Balanced Assessment Consortium (SBAC, 2010). The assessments will be based on universal design principles, and assessors will have the ability to adapt the computer-delivered test to meet the specific accommodations of students with diverse learning needs (Cortiella, n.d.). It is expected that these computer-based assessments will reduce the stigma associated with test modifications and provide teachers and parents with timely results for more efficient information on progress and instruction (Cortiella, n.d.). School leaders, teachers, and parents must work together to make the transition to the new CCSS assessments and the importance they will have on monitoring children's progress in grades K–3.

Research-Based Practical Tips and Caveats

Leaders should remember to do the following:

- Include families and community leaders in the decision-making process at the school level (e.g., school advisory councils).

- Meet with parents regularly about their understanding of and satisfaction with the CCSS.

- Encourage teachers and related service personnel to make home visits to keep parents informed of their child's progress on the CCSS and to find ways to connect the child's life experiences with the classroom curriculum.

- Ensure that time is available during the day for collaboration and planning between K–3 general teachers, special education teachers, and related service personnel.

- Understand the need for balance in the early years between developmentally appropriate practices and academics.

- Build expertise in K–3 and special education teachers to deconstruct the standards so that they have strong grounding in English/language arts and mathematics across the content areas.

- Provide resources to teachers for making appropriate accommodations/modification for children with disabilities, including assistive technology.

- Support implementation of a multi-tiered model to support the varying needs of young children with and without disabilities.

- Provide technology to teachers to support instructional decision making (e.g., data) and implementation of instruction.

- Support progress-monitoring systems for formative assessment of grade-level standards.

- Create communities of practice that explore evidence-based practices for young children with disabilities.

- Provide focused feedback on K–3 teachers by encouraging self-ratings, walkthroughs, observations, cueing teaching, and student surveys.

- Offer ongoing professional development activities that include workshops, online modules, book study groups, mentoring, and coaching with performance feedback.

- Implement a technology plan aimed at providing K–3 teachers with ongoing training on technology related to assessment and instruction.

- Connect with K–3 university teacher education programs to provide expertise in evidence-based instructional and assessment practices for young children with disabilities.

Summary

This chapter has outlined the importance of involving families in their child's education and how school leaders can facilitate the home–school relationship. Additionally, it is clear that implementing the CCSS in the early school years is important for providing the foundational skills that children will need later to be college- and career-ready. The balance between academics and social development in the early years continues to be a challenge for K–2 teachers. However, several evidence-based instructional strategies in language arts and mathematics within multi-tiered systems of support have been identified that will assist teachers in finding the balance. School leaders must support teachers and other school personnel in implementing high-quality curriculum, instruction, and assessments that support the integration of the CCSS in the classroom. The ultimate responsibility for ensuring that children master the knowledge and skills in the standards rests with school leaders, teachers, families, and the community.

This chapter began with Katie's journey from traumatic brain injury to life as a first grader in a small rural school. Her life away from school is filled with the sensory experiences of a farm—animals, farm machinery, crops of cotton and corn. Let's step now into her school setting—small school with moderate resources, but with teachers who understand and embrace the work ethic of life-on-the-farm. As we look at Katie's needs, we should first be drawn to the phrase, *moderate learning impairments in language, memory, and attention*. So, what should be the expected response of the classroom teacher to these children? And, how do school leaders address this issue? The classroom teacher can make those reasonable accommodations. *Requiring instructionally sound practices for a disabled child under your care keeps the legal wolves from your door, and besides, it is the right thing to do.*

We know neither the intensity nor duration of services that Katie will need as she progresses, but we do know that they start with a caring teacher who is profoundly knowledgeable in teaching reading—a teacher who knows not just how to identify a reading problem but more importantly how to help kids who struggle with acquiring those very complex reading skills. Let's start right there.

It takes a village to educate young children with disabilities like Katie. Her family, teachers, school administrators, and community are essential in assuring her success in kindergarten and beyond.

Note

1 In this chapter, we use the term early childhood teacher to describe teachers of children in K–3 settings.

References

Anderson, K., Harrison, T., & Lewis, K. (2012). *Plans to adopt and implement Common Core State Standards in the southeast region states.* Washington, DC: U.S. Department of Education, Institute of Education Sciences. Retrieved from http://ies.ed.gov/ncee/edlabs

Bryant, D. P., Bryant, B. R., Gersten, R. M., Scammacca, N. N., Funk, C., Winter, A., . . . Pool, C. (2008). The effects of tier 2 intervention on the mathematics performance of first-grade students who are at risk for mathematics difficulties. *Learning Disability Quarterly, 31*, 47–63.

Carnine, D. W., Silbert, J., Kame'enui, E. J., & Tarver, S. G. (2004). *Direct instruction reading* (4th ed.). Upper Saddle River, NJ: Pearson.

Cashman, J., Linehan, P., & Rosser, M. (2007). *Communities of Practice: A new approach to solving complex educational problems.* Alexandria, VA: National Association of State Directors of Special Education.

Cavanagh, S. (2012). Standards backers seek out support of parents. *Education Week, 32*(5), 13–15.

Clarke, B., Smolkowski, K., Baker, S. K., Fien, H., Doabler, C. T., & Chard, D. J. (2011). The impact of a comprehensive tier I core kindergarten program on the achievement of students at risk in mathematics. *Elementary School Journal, 111*, 561–584.

Cortiella, C. (n.d.). *Common Core perspective: The positive impact for kids with LD.* New York, NY: National Center for Learning Disabilities. Retrieved from http://www.ncld.org/students-disabilities/common-core-standards/common-core-perspective-positive-impact-for-kids-with-ld

Courtade, G., Spooner, F., Browder, D., & Jimenez, B. (2012). Seven reasons to promote standards-based instruction for students with severe disabilities: A reply to Ayres, Lowrey, Douglas, & Sievers (2011). *Education and Training in Autism and Developmental Disabilities, 47*(1), 3–13.

DeLorenzo, J. P. (2014, June). Curriculum instruction toward the Common Core learning standards. *New York State Education Department.* Retrieved from http://www.p12.nysed.gov/specialed/commoncore/instructionCCLS-parents-614.htm#att3

Doabler, C. T., Fien, H., Nelson-Walker, N. J., & Baker, S. K. (2012). Evaluating three elementary mathematics programs for presence of eight research-based instructional design principles. *Learning Disability Quarterly, 35*, 200–211.

Doabler, C. T., Nelson, N. J., Kosty, D. B., Fien, H., Baker, S. K., Smolkowski, K., & Clarke, B. (2014). Examining teachers' use of evidence-based practices during core mathematics instruction. *Assessment for Effective Intervention, 39*, 99–111. doi:10.1177/1534508413511848

Duncan, G. J., Dowsett, C. J., Claessens, A., Magnuson, K., Huston, A. C., Klebanov, P., . . . Japel, C. (2007). School readiness and later achievement. *Developmental Psychology, 43*, 1428–1446.

Elish-Piper, L. (2013). Parent involvement in reading. *Illinois Reading Council Journal, 41*(3), 56–59.

Fuchs, L. S., & Vaughn, S. (2012). Responsiveness-to-intervention: A decade later. *Journal of Learning Disabilities, 45*, 195–203. doi:10.1177/0022219412442150

Gallant, P. A. (2009). Kindergarten teachers speak out: "Too much, too soon, too fast!" *Reading Horizons, 49*, 201–220.

Gamm, S., Elliott, J., Wright Halbert, J., Price-Baugh, R., Hall, R., Walston, D., . . . Casserly, M. (2012). *Common Core State Standards and diverse urban students: Using multi-tiered systems of support.* Washington, DC: Council of Great City Schools. Retrieved from http://www.cgcs.org/domain/87

Graue, E. (2009). Reimagining kindergarten: Restoring a developmental approach when accountability demands are pushing formal instruction on the youngest learners. *School Administrator, 66*, 10–15.

Heitin, L. (2014, March 4). Teachers may need to deepen assessment practices for Common Core. *Education Week*. Retrieved from http://www.edweek.org/tm/articles/2014/03/05/ndia_formativeassessment.html

Houchens, G., & Cabrera, J. (2013). Preparing principals for instructional leadership: Integrating the Common Core standards—RESEARCH. *Kentucky Journal of Excellence in College Teaching and Learning, 11*, Article 7. Retrieved from http://encompass.eku.edu/kjectl/vol11/iss1/7

Kamps, D., Abbott, M., Greenwood, C., Wills, H., Veerkamp, M., & Kaufman, J. (2008). Effects of small-group reading instruction and curriculum differences for students most at risk in kindergarten: Two-year results for secondary- and tertiary-level interventions. *Journal of Learning Disabilities, 41*, 101–114. doi:10.1177/0022219407313412

Kent, S. C., Wanzek, J., & Al Otaiba, S. (2012). Print reading in general education kindergarten classrooms: What does it look like for students at-risk for reading difficulties? *Learning Disabilities Research & Practice, 27*, 56–65.

Kober, N., & Rentner, D. S. (2012). *Year two of implementing the Common Core State Standards: States' progress and challenges*. Washington, DC: Center on Education Policy. Retrieved from http://files.eric.ed.gov/fulltext/ED528907.pdf

Kramer-Vida, L., Levitt, R., & Kelly, S. P. (2012). Kindergarten is more than ready for the Common Core State Standards. *Language Arts, 90*, 93–109.

Lynch, S., & Adams, P. (2008). Developing standards-based individualized education program objectives for students with significant needs. *TEACHING Exceptional Children, 40*(3), 36–39.

Main, L. K. (2012). Too much too soon? Common Core math standards in the early years. *Early Childhood Education Journal, 40*, 73–77. doi:10.1007/s10643-011-0484-7

Morgan, J. J., Brown, N. B., Hsiao, Y.-J., Howrter, C., Juniel, P., Sedano, L., . . . Castillo, W. L. (2014, January). Unwrapping academic standards to increase the achievement of students with disabilities. *Intervention in School and Clinic, 49*(3), 131–141. doi:10.1177/1053451213496156

National Association for the Education of Young Children (NAEYC) & National Association of Early Childhood Specialists in State Departments of Education (NAECS-SDE). (2010). *Joint statement of the National Association for the Education of Young Children and the National Association of the Early Childhood Specialists in State Departments of Education on the Common Core standards initiative related to kindergarten through third grade*. Washington, DC: NAEYC & NAECS-SDE. Retrieved from https://www.naeyc.org/store/?gclid=CJGthM7Ku8g-CFVYUHwodAOMCGQ

National PTA. (n.d.). *Common Core video series—Advocacy*. Retrieved from http://www.pta.org/ccssvideos

Neuman, S. B., & Roskos, K. (2013). Why Common Core matters? What parents need to know? *The Reading Teacher, 67*(1), 9–11. doi:10.1002/TRTR.1186

Nick, F. (2014). *Involving parents in the Common Core State Standards: Through a family school partnership program*. Bloomington, IN: Xlibris LLC.

Partnership for the Assessment of Readiness for College and Careers. (2014). *About PARCC*. Retrieved from http://www.parcconline.org/about-parcc

Pretti-Frontczak, K. (2014). Stop trying to make kids "ready" for kindergarten. *Young Exceptional Children, 17*, 51–53. doi:10.1177/1096250614523346

Problem Solving & Response to Intervention Project, Florida's Positive Behavior Support Project, & University of South Florida. (2011). *MTSS implementation components:*

Ensuring common language and understanding. Retrieved from http://flpbs.fmhi.usf.edu/pdfs/MTSS%20Paper%20Impl%20Comp%20Dec%202011.pdf

Robbins, T., Stagman, S., & Smith, S. (2012, October). *Young children at risk: National and state prevalence of risk factors* (Fact Sheet). New York, NY: National Center for Children in Poverty. Retrieved from www.nccp.org/publications/pdf/text_1073.pdf

SMARTER Balanced Assessment Consortium (SBAC). (2010). *Latest news.* Retrieved from http://www.smarterbalanced.org/

Spencer, E. J., Goldstein, H., & Kaminski, R. (2012). Teaching vocabulary in storybooks: Embedding explicit vocabulary instruction for young children. *Young Exceptional Children, 15*(1), 18–32. doi:10.1177/1096250611435367

Willhoft, J. (2012). Leading the way. *Principal Leadership, 13*(4), 19–21.

Zwiers, J., O'Hara, S., & Pritchard, R. (2014). *Common Core standards in diverse classrooms: Essential practices for developing academic language & disciplinary literacy.* Portsmouth, NH: Stenhouse.

CHAPTER

5

English Learners

It's More Than Getting an Interpreter

Diane Rodriguez and Gloria D. Campbell-Whatley

Jesus is in middle school and lives in an urban environment. He moved here from Spain last year and his parents know very little English. His home life is unstable. He runs away from school when he is frustrated and does not meet academic benchmarks. He receives English language learner services, and the teacher provides a number of activities that he has difficulty completing independently. He gets along well with the other students and operates well in cooperative learning groups. His teacher has tried a number of interventions and has decided that if she got him placed in special education he would get the extra help he needed. There has been little success getting an interpreter and she doesn't know what he is saying half of the time. The school has so many needs and has a 70 percent free and reduced population. The teacher has 30 students per hour for five hours each school day. Though exasperated with the school system, the teacher wants to help Jesus. In addition to seeking a special education placement, the teacher wonders whether focusing Jesus on attainment of particular CCSS would work for him.

Introduction

The large number of English language learners (ELLs) in America's classrooms continues to grow and has increased by 65 percent, causing greater demand for English as a second language (ESL) programs and services. Unfortunately, systemic issues continue to diminish scholastic opportunities for culturally and linguistically diverse learners, but teachers can alleviate some hardship by addressing particular issues within their classrooms. Many critical issues pertaining to ELLs pertain to instructional standards and assessment, as related to culture. There is an acute need to integrate cultural literature into disciplines as well as accommodate language differences and cultural nuances, especially in the core curriculum and standards-based instruction. Sometimes ESL instruction is considered a separate entity from standard-based instruction, but ESL activities should be infused into the classroom curriculum.

Assessment of ELLs is another major concern. At times, ELLs are excluded from tests, and when included, they are often expected to participate in assessments that make inaccurate assumptions about language proficiency and content knowledge. Another key concern is inattention to culture. In many classes, content is not connected to the students' background, which day after day becomes exceedingly dispiriting for ELLs as they earnestly seek to attain instructional goals. Collectively, these issues and the additional label applied to ELLs receiving special services render traditional instructional methods ineffective. This chapter focuses on these issues and remedies available to K–12 teachers and special education leaders. All teachers and leaders are responsible for all students and, therefore, accountable for helping all students attain the CCSS in the vast majority of states (Calderón, 2014).

Defining and Closing Language Differences

The overarching goal of bilingual education is to educate learners meaningfully in two languages, enabling them to function across cultures (Garcia & Kleifgen, 2010). Language is an important aspect of bilingual education. The pedagogical emphasis is to utilize language to gain content knowledge for academic success in two languages. ELLs with and without disabilities benefit from instruction in two languages as they build content knowledge. For ELLs attaining the CCSS and applying their knowledge, intensive instruction in two languages is very beneficial. The CCSS require stronger literacy skills than past standards, and for many ELLs and other students, the language demands are especially challenging (Heitin, 2014). Bunch, Kibler, and Pimentel (2012) stated, "Language development and cognitive development are interrelated and mutually dependent; ELLs learn language as they learn content" (p. 2).

According to Maxwell (2012), many states are developing English language proficiency standards to clarify for teachers the sophisticated language skills that their students will need to succeed within the rigorous new CCSS expectations. Kinsella (2012) offers strategies to prepare adolescent English learners for the cultural and linguistic demands of academic interactions. She proposes the following provisions: (a) appropriate instructional supports to make grade-level course work comprehensible, (b) additional time to complete tasks and assessments, (c) opportunities for classroom interactions that develop concepts and academic language in the disciplines, and (d) opportunities to interact with proficient English speakers.

Language arts as a school subject area is conceptualized as a deliberate curriculum that includes the development of students' listening, speaking, reading, and writing skills and processes through a prescribed set of language and literacy experiences in order to prepare them to become lifelong literate and academically successful adults and citizens. The current language arts curriculum in many schools has been greatly influenced by the standards-based education reform movement in the United States, which is developing a set of "common learning outcomes," expectations, or "standards" that are basic and necessary to all students and measured through standardized grade-level assessments. Learning standards are statements that express what students ought to know or what they should be capable of doing at particular points in their learning progression. A complete set of standards is directed toward the attainment of a general goal, and these standards are used by schools to guide instruction. The language arts curriculum must follow grade-level goals/standards, which identify expectations for attaining particular knowledge and capabilities in language arts courses (National Government Association Center for Best Practices & Council of Chief State School Officers, 2010). These language and literacy expectations are often called "learning standards." The emphasis for the language arts curriculum is on literacy learning across the curriculum, focusing on cognitive skills such as problem formulation, research investigation, and interpretation of communication. School principals and teachers agree that learning standards do not dictate the content of the language arts instruction; learning standards are meant to be used as a guide in the development of learning experiences. For example, learning standards guide bilingual teachers as they plan to instruct bilingual students in first or second language. While discussing the application of the CCSS to ELLs, the National Government Association Center for Best Practices and Council of Chief State School Officers (2010) stated the need for rigorous grade-level expectations in the areas of speaking, listening, reading, and writing in order to prepare all students, including ELLs, to be college- and career-ready. Second-language learners will also benefit from learning how to negotiate settings where they are able to participate on equally with native speakers in all aspects of social, economic, and civic endeavors. ELLs who are literate in a first language can apply first-language vocabulary knowledge when reading in English.

Although the CCSS view the native language as an additive factor in ELL acquisition and development, and not as an enhancement of the students' native language in itself, the National Government Association Center for Best Practices and the Council of Chief State School Officers clearly recognize the importance of native language literacy and background knowledge in bilingual students' learning and academic development. Teachers should have these standards in mind and recognize the value of each student's native language when planning instruction for the development of language and literacy. These sets of learning expectations guide attainment of language arts in both English and the native language. When language arts instruction is provided in the first language, recognition is given to the student's facility with his or her primary language, facilitating inclusion of students' prior knowledge, culture, and perspectives. In addition to the general expectations required in the area of language and literacy, there is a set of expectations related to students' grade-level achievement. The native language grade-level curriculum is designed to help bilingual students become independent learners. In practical terms, independent learners exhibit the ability to:

- comprehend and evaluate texts;
- construct effective arguments;
- ask relevant questions;
- listen and respond;
- demonstrate command of the oral language;
- use a wide range of grade-level vocabulary;
- use resources to assist in learning; and
- demonstrate learning through a variety of individual products.

Bunch et al. (2012) recommend consideration of students' second language proficiency, literacy backgrounds, and background knowledge to inform instructional efforts, especially when called upon to read texts beyond their English language proficiency levels. Furthermore, Rodríguez, Carrasquillo, and Kyung (2014) recommend that teachers encourage ELL students to draw upon their native language to help them comprehend, analyze, and evaluate information.

Instruction and CCSS

Boyd-Batstone (2013) define strategies for school leaders and teachers to help ELLs meet the CCSS. The language behaviors of ELL learners will first need to be recognized:

- Part of the learning strategy of ELLs is to actively listen, so they may be silent for a portion of the learning experience. The silent behavior is indicative of and should be acknowledged as a part of the student's culture. Teachers should be mindful of this behavior and allow time for the student to work through this phase.
- When speaking to ELL students voice modulation is important. People tend to automatically speak louder when someone does not appear to understand English. A louder voice can be distressing to the ELL and they might interpret the increase in volume as chastisement.

English Learners: It's More Than Getting an Interpreter

- It is important to use concrete objects and demonstration techniques during instruction with ELLs. Pictures, objects, and diagrams give meaning to the context. Visual, auditory, kinesthetic, tactile (VAKT—learning styles-based teaching focuses on using the senses for instructional) methods activate comprehension and memory and are strongly suggested for this population.

- Dramatizing or acting out a skill or concept or the use of a visual provides more meaning to the ELL.

- Assure ELLs that it is alright for them to use their native language. Use of their own language provides a bridge for them to better understand English.

- CCSS require informational texts, but many of these can be chosen by the teacher. Choose texts that ELLs want to read. Texts that provide captions, illustrations, pronunciation of key words are better selections for ELLs.

Table 5.1 provides clues for administration of the CCSS speaking and listening standards that strengthen the application of the above strategies (Boyd-Batstone, 2013).

Lee, Quinn, and Valdes (2013) propose that the language demands of CCSS will negatively affect ELLs and particularly in science and engineering. They suggest that content area courses be taught by teachers who have training in instructing the ELL. Teachers will need to focus on academic content as well as language objectives and Science.

In their research, they demonstrate that math, English and language arts (E/LA), and science intersect and all require (a) acquiring knowledge through texts, (b) reading, writing, and speaking, (c) engaging and constructing arguments, (d) constructing explanations, (e) evaluating and communicating information, (f) synthesizing and reporting findings, etc. Leaders will need to examine:

- science and engineering practices that are occurring in the classroom;

- the assessment of the constructs, concepts, and language in science;

Table 5.1 Speaking and Listening CCSS for ELL Students

Grade	Standards and Instructional Suggestions
K–2	To help students understand one- to two-step directions, use appropriate voice modulation, and dramatize or act out directions and appropriate expected responses to a given assignment
3–4	To help ELLs follow rules for a planned discussion and listening to others; teachers should allow students to use pictures or diagrams during the discussion
6–8	If ELLs need to set goals and guidelines for a discussion for this standard, then they will most likely be successful if the group is arranged in a format that includes role assignment. For example, a note-taker, a leader, etc., will provide the structure needed. Of course, visuals are always appropriate and can strengthen the interactions
9–12	Presenting a discussion with alternative views (i.e., democratic discussions, informal, having informal consensus, deciding on key issues) will require the teacher to use appropriate voice modulation, visuals and group activities to help ELLs succeed

- the assessment of science and engineering instruction as ELLs progress through grade levels;

- the supports in place for language in science and engineering classrooms; and

- technologies and tools used that are appropriate for ELL students in science and engineering classes.

School Challenges and Solutions: Smoothing Rough Places

What can leaders do to understand school environmental challenges and to devise solutions for effective learning for ELLs? Researchers and practitioners have considered that question and their recommendations are helpful. Particularly useful are Culturally Responsive Classroom Management (CRCM) strategies developed by the Metropolitan Center for Urban Education and New York University's Steinhardt School of Culture, Education and Human Development. CRCM is a pedagogical approach designed to guide leaders to management decisions (Metropolitan Center for Urban Education, 2008). Leaders will need to devise training that helps teachers:

- to recognize their own cultural lens and biases;

- to know of the cultural backgrounds of students;

- to be aware of the broader social, economic, and political contexts of language;

- to increase or create the ability and willingness to use culturally appropriate management strategies; and

- to commit to building caring classroom communities and schools.

The following recommendations from Coleman and Goldenberg (2012) are also beneficial. Leaders must ensure that teachers provide:

- appropriate instructional supports to make grade-level course work comprehensible;

- modified assessments that allow ELLs to demonstrate their content knowledge;

- additional time for ELLs to complete tasks and assessments;

- opportunities for classroom interactions (both listening and speaking) that develop concepts and academic language in the disciplines;

- opportunities for ELLs to interact with proficient English speakers;

- opportunities for ELLs to build on their strengths, prior experiences, and background knowledge; and

- effective practices (Common Core State Standards Initiative, 2010).

School-Based Leaders

School leaders have tremendous challenges to determining professional development because of the proliferation of languages in K–12 settings. For example, the Washington school district has 138 spoken languages, and in a class of 24, 18 of the students come from homes that speak different languages (Schachter, 2013). It is suggested that teachers and leaders obtain certification in ELL, especially where there are large numbers of ELLs in the school district. Language differences can no longer be viewed as problematic, but rather as a resource to increase appreciation and skills in working with other cultures; therefore, Schachter (2013) suggest the following:

- Collaborating among English-speaking and ESL teachers to create CCSS higher level thinking, problem solving, and inquiry-based lessons and projects that ELLs can learn and understand.

- Using differentiated instruction during lessons; at the same time having ESL students and native speakers work together using an inquiry-based approach (see Chapter 9) with hands-on activities.

- Creating classroom-based group projects where students can develop an understanding of the language.

- Using activities during and after school to assist with English development for ELLs.

- Heavily involving the parents of ELLs during and after-school activities.

- Using translators for communication and correspondence with parents.

- Using formative assessment for language and content learning that provides alternative ways for students to show knowledge of CCSS standards, deemphasizing linguistics and emphasizing knowledge of the standard.

Special Education Leaders

Special education leaders are going to determine if ELL students really have a disability or if there are language differences. There have been court cases, as far back as 1970, such as *Diana vs the Board of Education*, where ELLs were placed in special education and identified with a disability, yet actually there was only a language difference (McLean, 1995). Therefore, special education leaders must ensure that educators understand the differences between *language differences* and *language disorders* (Ortiz & Artiles, 2010). Klingner and Eppolito (2014) found similarities

Table 5.2 Some Similarities in ELLs and Students with Disabilities

Behaviors Associated with Acquiring a Second Language	Behaviors Associated with Having a Learning Disability
Challenges following directions	Challenges following directions
Challenges distinguishing between sounds that are not in a native language	Challenges with phonological awareness
Confusion with sound-symbol and pronouncing that are not in their native language	Slow to learn sound-symbol correspondence
Challenges remembering sight words without the attached word meaning	Challenges remembering sight words
May understand more than what can be conveyed in one's native language	Challenges retelling a story in sequence

between students with disabilities and ELLs such as (a) confusion with figurative language, (b) slow to process challenging language, (c) poor auditory memory, (d) difficulty concentrating, and (e) becoming easily frustrated. Some differences between ELLs and learners with disabilities are presented in Table 5.2, which may provide some insights into why ELLs are significantly overrepresented in special education. Leaders need to note that many factors must be considered and eliminated as possible reasons for a student's struggle.

Applying the Common Core Standards and Solutions

Challenging standards for students and high expectations can also have a positive effect on changing educator's practices and increasing student achievement (August et al., 2008). Calderón (2014) discusses teaching the CCSS for ELLs through explicit:

- teaching of academic language/vocabulary for discourse, reading, and writing;

- instruction on reading in all subjects; and

- writing instruction by preteaching important vocabulary, developing background knowledge, and describing, modeling, and supporting the writing.

All students should be held to the same high expectations outlined in the CCSS, including ELLs; however, these students may require additional time, appropriate instructional support, and aligned assessments (van Lier & Walqui, 2012). It is important to recognize that the development of native-like proficiency in English takes many years. Accordingly, ELLs who start schooling in the United States in later grades will need additional time to meet the language arts standards.

Leaders need to realize that as ELLs seek to meet the language standards in English proficiency planning, preparing and selecting appropriate grade-level texts and vocabulary strategies are a necessity. During reading, ESL interactive reading methods should be used. For example, the questioning strategies and

Table 5.3 Language and ELLs

Language advancements	Acquisition of discipline-specific language
Language encumbrances	Language expectations embedded informational texts and assignments
Language framework	Instructional strategies to help students gain access to concepts
Language provisions	Organize to support students in understanding language and content

differentiated instruction are discussed in Chapter 9. Universal Design for Learning strategies are also apropos (discussed in Chapter 8).

Calderón (2014) and August et al. (2008) suggest teaching ELLs principal word learning strategies using word parts, recognizing and using cognates for speakers whose first language shares cognates with English. Additional strategies pertain to the use of context, grammar, word morphology, punctuation, world knowledge, surrounding discourse and text, and word association. Teachers should allow students to use bilingual dictionaries and focus on vocabulary building with meaningful activities centered on texts. These strategies will help ELLs perform in the CCSS. Santos, Darling-Hammond, and Cheuk (2012) suggest a few issues that need to be addressed for ELLs (Table 5.3).

Connection to Assessment

Abedi and Levine (2013) speak to the necessity of adaptations of the Smarter Balanced Assessment Consortium (SBAC) and the Partnership for the Assessment of Readiness for College and Career (PARCC) for ELLs to provide an equal assessment opportunity. Many of the accommodations in place are not considered as valid and are inappropriate for serving the needs of ELLs (Abedi & Levine, 2013). For example, linguistic structure of the questions on the test may not actually be acquiring what the ELLs might really know, because the test requires a high level of language proficiency for adequate performance such as explaining, constructing arguments, critiquing, writing, speaking, and listening that require high levels of understanding in English, even for those who are not ELLs! To adjust linguistic accessibility, modifications will need to focus on the context of the task rather than the linguistic demands to appropriately answer the question. Heitin (2014) writes that there are some states providing accommodations and alignment for SBAC and PARCC such as the use of glossaries and read-aloud text-to-speech modifications for *some* portions of the test and *some* grade levels, but these provisions are not viewed as "enough" to level the play field. For example, if you use some options like text-to-speech, then the results include a disclaimer about reading abilities.

Formative measures should be used to assess bilingual emergent learners to determine where the students are academically on a continuum. It is a necessity to track the success of instructional strategies and interventions. It is recommended that teachers assess proficiency in the second language and native language of the student in speaking, listening, reading, and writing both formally and informally.

Authentic assessment provides a valid picture of the strengths of bilingual emergent learners (Abedi & Levine, 2013).

Gewertz (2013) presents a good model for leaders implementing the CCSS. He presents a learning cycle that includes a six- to eight-week instructional unit. As a teacher instructs, ELL coaches work with them individually and in groups. The coaches observe, co-teach, provide feedback, and work on plans for improvement. At the end of the learning cycle, an interim assessment is given to students. After scoring the assessments, teachers, coaches, and leaders use a professional development day in school teams, analyzing the test results and planning ways to reteach needed areas. Then they focus on academic disciplines, such as "close reading" of complex text in EL/A. Afterward, a new learning cycle begins and teachers incorporate the information learned into the new instruction.

The manner in which native language and English are incorporated into instruction for ELLs is vital. As Soltero-González, Escamilla, and Hopewell (2010) stated, "the coexistence of two or more languages in young children contributes to a uniquely endowed human being whose experiences and knowledge can never be measured or understood as independently constrained by each language separately" (p. 224). Therefore, it is necessary to ensure that after teachers use a repertoire of assessment tools to measure academic knowledge and skills of emergent bilingual learners with disabilities, the teachers provide instruction appropriate for their ELLs. Use of fair assessments is vital. Leaders choosing assessment practices will need to (Garcia & Kleifgen, 2010):

- determine equitable assessment practices for bilingual learners;
- know the relationship between academic learning for ELLs and content proficiency;
- determine the validity of high-stakes tests for this population;
- determine what assessments matches the population of students; and
- assist teachers in the interpretation of assessments of student learning which are essential for growth.

Garcia and Kleifgen (2010), Herrera, Murry, and Morales-Cabral (2007), and Ortiz and Artiles (2010) recommend using multiple types of assessments and testing accommodations in order to provide an accurate conception of student learning. For example, leaders may provide accommodations for bilingual learners with disabilities that include:

- presentation of content;
- student responses in their native and second language;
- timing and scheduling of the assessments; and
- reinforcement of resources available for these students.

Research-Based Tips and Caveats

- The number of ELLs has increased by 65%, causing greater demand for ESL programs and services.

- ESL instruction should be infused into regular classroom instruction.

- ELLs need appropriate instructional supports, additional time to complete assignments and assessments, and opportunities for classroom interactions with proficient English speakers.

- ELLs should be encouraged to use their native language to help them comprehend, analyze, and evaluate information.

- Math, EL/A and science intersect and require reading, writing, and speaking, constructing arguments, and synthesizing and reporting findings. Creating, adapting, and monitoring science and engineering instruction, assessment practices, supports, and technologies that are appropriate for ELLs in science and engineering classes are paramount.

- English-speaking and ESL teachers need to collaborate in order to craft CCSS higher level inquiry-based lessons and projects.

- ESLs and native speakers should work together using inquiry-based approaches with hands-on activities.

- Special education leaders will need to differentiate between language differences and disability.

- Garcia and Kleifgen (2010), Herrera et al. (2007), and Ortiz and Artiles (2010) recommend using multiple types of assessments and testing accommodations to provide an accurate conception of student learning.

- ELLs should be held to the same high expectations in the CCSS with additional time, instructional support, and aligned assessments (van Lier & Walqui, 2012), and especially those who come to the United States in middle and high school.

- Leaders and teachers need to be certified in ESL if there are large ELL populations in their districts.

Summary

As we began this chapter, we met Jesus and his teacher, Mr. Verbal. Both were experiencing problems not uncommon in today's school: (a) a student who speaks limited English with parents who have even less understanding of English with instability at home to add to the issues; and (b) a teacher, Mr. Verbal, who cares about Jesus but lacks specific knowledge about how to proceed especially since he has 29 other students in Jesus's class.

The implementation of the CCSS will affect the instructional practices, curriculum, and language proficiency for ELLs across the country (Lee et al., 2013). As the population of ELLs continue to grow in the United States, it is vital that states and districts focus more attention on effectively preparing educators to serve the distinct needs of this population. Teachers should know the essential information for addressing the needs of ELLs with and without disabilities. For instance, lots of independent seatwork without teacher guidance is not a good technique for Jesus, or for any students. The support of oral language is key to effective teaching for ELLs. Mr. Verbal's thoughts about referring Jesus for a disability for additional support are a bit off-base in that deficiency in English is not a disability under the law. However, it may be that Jesus has a disability in both his native language and English, and the only way to determine that is with a referral.

Mr. Verbal is typical of most teachers with no ESL training. They are unconsciously incompetent about ESL strategies. That is—they don't know what they don't know, and they are left to experiment. While unconscious incompetence about ELLs is not a teacher's fault, in the interest of equity, school districts must ensure that all teachers are adequately prepared to work with ELLs. Because each school is at least semiautonomous, the task of bringing all teachers to conscious competence about ELL strategies is a major function of leadership that will revolve around educating and certifying content teachers to serve ELLs. To help cross these barriers, collaboration among teachers is a necessity. Jesus needs teachers who care and who work together, but he also needs a principal who will not stop until language as a barrier to learning is eliminated.

References

Abedi, J., & Levine, H. G. (2013). Fairness in assessment of English learners. *Leadership, 42*(3), 26–38.

August, D., Beck, I. L., Calderón, M., Francis, D. J., Lesaux, N. K., & Shanahan, T. (2008). Instruction and professional development. In D. August & T. Shanahan (Eds.), *Developing reading and writing in second language learners: Lessons from the report of the national literacy panel on language-minority children and youth.* London, England: Routledge.

Boyd-Batstone, P. (2013). Five strategies to help ELLs meet the Common Core. *California Reader, 47*(1), 27–31.

Bunch, G. C., Kibler, A., & Pimentel, S. (2012). *Realizing opportunities for English learners in the Common Core English language arts and disciplinary literacy standards.* Paper presented at the Understanding Language Conference at Stanford University, Stanford, CA. Retrieved from http://ell.stanford.edu/sites/default/files/pdf/academic-papers/01_Bunch_Kibler_Pimentel_RealizingOpp%20in%20ELA_FINAL_0.pdf

Calderón, M. E. (2014, February). Teaching across the board. *Language Magazine, 13*(6), 18. Retrieved from http://languagemagazine.com/?page_id=29732

Coleman, R., & Goldenberg, C. (2012, February). The Common Core challenge for English language learners. *Principal Leadership,* 46–51.

Common Core State Standards Initiative. (2010). *Application of Common Core State Standards for English language learners.* Retrieved from http://www.corestandards.org/assets/application-for-english-learners.pdf

Garcia, O., & Kleifgen, J. (2010). *Educating emergent bilinguals: Policies, programs, and practices for English language learners.* New York, NY: Teachers College Press.

Gewertz, C. (2013). District bets big on standards. *Education Week, 32*(32), 1–10.

Heitin, L. (2014). Testing plans differ on accommodations. *Education Week, 33*(29), 530–533.

Herrera, S., Murry, K., & Morales-Cabral, R. (2007). *Assessment and accommodations for classroom teachers of culturally and linguistically diverse students.* Boston, MA: Pearson.

Kinsella, K. (2012, December). Communicating on the same wavelength. *Language Magazine, 12*(4), 18–25.

Klingner, J., & Eppolito, A. (2014). *English language learners: Differentiating between language acquisition and learning disabilities.* Reston, VA. Council for Exceptional Children.

Lee, O., Quinn, H., & Valdés, G. (2013). Science and language for English language learners in relation to next generation science standards and with implications for Common Core State Standards for English language arts and mathematics. *Educational Researchers, 42*(4), 223–233.

Maxwell, L. A. (2012, October). Guide advises on trying English proficiency to Common Core. *Education Week, 32*(7), 6–7.

McLean, Z. Y. (1995). History of bilingual assessment and its impact on best practices used today. *New York State Association for Bilingual Education Journal, 10*, 6–12.

Metropolitan Center for Urban Education. (2008). *Culturally responsive classroom management strategies.* New York, NY: NYU Steinhardt.

National Government Association Center for Best Practices & Council of Chief State School Officers. (2010). *National governors' association and state education chiefs launch common state academic standards.* Retrieved from http://www.ccsso.org/News_and_Events/Press_Releases/NATIONAL_GOVERNORS_ASSOCIATION_AND_STATE_EDUCATION_CHIEFS_LAUNCH_COMMON_STATE_ACADEMIC_STANDARDS_.html

Ortiz, A., & Artiles, A. J. (2010). Meeting the needs of English language learners with disabilities: A linguistically and culturally responsive model. In G. Li & P. Edwards (Eds.), *Best practices in ELL instruction* (pp. 247–272). New York, NY: Guilford.

Rodríguez, D., Carrasquillo, A., & Kyung, S. L. (2014). *The bilingual advantage: Promoting English learners' academic development and biliteracy through native language instruction.* New York, NY: Teachers College Press.

Santos, M., Darling-Hammond, L., & Cheuk, T. (2012). *Teacher development to support English language learners in the context of Common Core State Standards.* Paper presented at the Understanding Language Conference at Stanford University, Stanford, CA. Retrieved from http://ell.stanford.edu/sites/default/files/pdf/academic-papers/10-Santos%20LDH%20Teacher%20Development%20FINAL.pdf

Schachter, R. (2013). Are schools getting tongue-tied? *District Administration, 49*(4), 57–60.

Soltero-González, L., Escamilla, K., & Hopewell, S. (2010). A bilingual perspective on writing assessment: Implications for teachers of emerging bilingual writers. In G. Li & P. A. Edwards (Eds.), *Best practices in ELL instruction* (pp. 222–244). New York, NY: Guilford Press.

van Lier, L., & Walqui, A. (2012). *Language and the Common Core State Standards.* Paper presented at the Understanding Language Conference at Stanford University, Stanford, CA. Retrieved from http://ell.stanford.edu/publication/language-and-common-core-state-standards

CHAPTER

Children in Urban Centers

*Gloria D. Campbell-Whatley, Keonya Booker,
Derrick Robinson, and Bettie Butler*

Jamal, an African-American male in the fifth grade, lives in an urban environment where the crime rate is very high. He is currently living with his aunt (father's sister), while his father is incarcerated. He is included in the general education setting and disrupts the entire class at least once a day. His math skills are well below grade level, but he reads fairly well. His Functional Behavior Assessment shows that he will respond in a confrontational manner to teacher directions or reprimands and has a hard time following classroom rules. He does not complete assignments and his in-class work is incomplete. He responds positively to music, sings well, composes songs and poems, and can play the piano, although he does not understand how to read music. He also demonstrates problem-solving and memory skills that are not evident in his courses. Can we integrate the CCSS and be sure this student is college- or career-ready?

Introduction

The educational challenge of the 21st century is to provide an equal opportunity of school success for all children. One-third of them have limited English proficiency and come from diverse backgrounds. According to "Racial/Ethnic Enrollment in Public Schools" (2015), one of three students enrolled in a public school is a student of racial or ethnic minority. One in five children under 18 live in poverty, and one in seven children between the ages of 5 and 17 speak a language other than English at home.

As more students from diverse ethnic, cultural, and social backgrounds enter public schools, leaders must provide an enriching learning environment that encourages academic equality and achievement. Such a learning environment would acknowledge the importance of integrating cultural and personal experiences that students bring with them to the classroom structure. The promise of effective infusion of culturally responsive instruction within special education classrooms provides students with greater chances for academic success; however, the challenge is to make it happen. How do we plan for students like Jamal and assure their academic needs are met while implementing the CCSS? This chapter will focus on school-based and special education leaders and the development of academic success in an urban climate.

Defining the Urban Environment: Concept and Construct

An urban school district is a school zone that has 70 percent or more urban schools. These schools are located in a city rather than a rural or suburban town. Urban school districts have a relatively high (a) rate of poverty as measured by free and reduced lunch data, (b) proportion of students of color, and (c) proportion of students with limited English proficiency (ESL) (Garza, 2009). Sixty-five million students are served in urban centers, and many of them are like Jamal described in the vignette.

The Word "Urban"

The most common conceptualization of *urban* is provided by the U.S. Census Bureau. For more than a century, this agency has established the criteria used to define an urban environment. The definition itself has varied over time in response to changes in settlement patterns, data usage, and available technology (http://quickfacts.census.gov/qfd/index.html).

Beginning in 1910, *urban* was formally defined by the Census Bureau (http://quickfacts.census.gov/qfd/index.html) as all territory, population, and housing units within an incorporated area that met the population threshold of 2,500 inhabitants. In 1950, this definition was expanded to reflect the growth in suburban areas outside the boundaries of incorporated places (http://quickfacts.census.gov/qfd/index.html). The term *urbanized area* was adopted and used to include large, densely populated, unincorporated areas of 50,000 or more residents. Following the 1950 Census, urban was redefined as all territory, persons, and housing units within an urbanized area and, *outside an urbanized area*, in all incorporated or unincorporated places, with 2,500 or more residents ("State and County Estimates for 1995," 1995).

Nearly 50 years later, with the emergence of the 2000 Census, the concept of urban was further expanded. The term *urban cluster* was introduced and used to refer to relatively small, densely settled territories of *at least 2,500 people but fewer than 50,000 people* (http://quickfacts.census.gov/qfd/index.html). Urban clusters were intended to substitute those places classified as urban with 2,500 or more persons located outside of urbanized areas. The integration of this term provided a more consistent and accurate measure of the population concentration in and around places (U.S. Department of Commerce, Economics and Statistics Administration, 2003).

Today, to qualify as an urban area, all territory, population, and housing units must be located within either an urbanized area or an urban cluster. The Census Bureau delineates urbanized areas and urban clusters exclusively using population density, which consists of: (a) surrounding block groups and census blocks with a population density of at least 500 people per square mile, and (b) a cluster of one or more block groups or census blocks with a population density of at least 1,000 people per square mile (U.S. Department of Commerce, Economics and Statistics Administration, 2003).

Despite wide acceptance, the Census Bureau's conceptualization of urban is limited, at best and at worst, completely arbitrary. Its generality and abstraction makes the definition both incomplete and insufficient for understanding the social context (i.e., those underlying characteristics and aspects that go beyond physical structures and geographical boundaries) of urban environments (Germani, 1973). As such, no true definition of urban can be fully achieved using measurements alone (Wirth, 1938), but instead consideration must also be given to the sociological construction of the concept.

What, then, does it mean to be urban? After some thought, Louis Wirth (1938), who is often cited for developing a logically coherent sociological definition of urbanism, postulates that to be urban means that a city, or social entity, may be defined as a reasonably large, densely populated, permanent living and settlement patterns of socially heterogeneous individuals. With this definition, Wirth calls attention to the inclusion of social groups as a major urban characteristic, which represents a departure from the Census Bureau's focus on numbers. Interestingly, by emphasizing the significance of social groups, the meaning of urban transcends conventional thought that exclusively ties urban to population density and, in turn, gives salience to human behavior and relationships.

Naturally, any given environment is going to be shaped by sociological factors which consider: (1) human relationships, (2) patterns of behavior, (3) perceptions of inequality, and (4) the nature of power. However, these factors are interpreted or constructed very differently based on experience, because the urban environment is often defined on the basis of marginalization. Therefore, to define urban, an understanding of patterns of behavior and social inequality is required.

Urban as a social construct returns attention to the importance of engagement and communication in social spaces. Interpreting how people behave and with whom they interact fosters a greater understanding of the nature of power and perceptions of marginal status within communities. Individual and collective experiences work together to shape and inform attitudes and beliefs about which groups are in control and which groups face exclusion. The word urban has numerous interpretations. To some it means a concentration of diverse populations and drums up the vision of "inner city streets plagued with poverty." Many suburbanites divide themselves and keep the issues of the city away from them; however, in some environs there is gentrification or urban renewal that is redefining the meaning of the word urban.

Defining the environment is a precursor for reflecting on the type of practices and strategies that leaders should be aware of in urban settings. The next section describes the ramifications of these environs related to instruction.

Culturally Relevant Pedagogy CCSS

Gloria Ladson-Billings (1995a) describes culturally relevant pedagogy (CPR) as "linking schooling with culture" (p. 159) to help students experience academic success, maintain cultural integrity, and become critical of the status quo. Strengths of CRP are observed in Ensign's (2003) assessment of its power to integrate students' lives as a basis of school work in order to become "Culturally Connected" (p. 414). Johnson (2011), in a three-year empirical study, indicates that teacher perceptions of self and others, social relations, and conception of knowledge are all positively impacted by the implementation of CRP. At the core of CRP is the notion that both teacher and student behavior is the result of culturally patterned behavior (Brown-Jeffy & Cooper, 2011). The authors go further to note five principles of CRP that range from identity development and acceptance of multiple perspectives to bridging home, school, and community as a way to strengthen social relations and classroom atmosphere.

Given the racial disparities in college access and achievement, it has become necessary that instructional practices embrace CRP "to get students to choose academic excellence" (Ladson-Billings, 1995a, p. 160). CRP proponents task teachers with linking home, school, and community (Brown-Jeffy & Cooper, 2011) to enable students to see their identities and cultures as strengths (Ladson-Billings, 1995a). While scholars can generally agree on the merit/sincerity of both CCSS and CRP, the challenge for schools will be integrating them into the instructional beliefs of the educator and institution. At the core of this challenge is navigating change. CCSS proposes to change the focus, rigor, and coherence of instructional delivery (Schmidt & Houang, 2012). This will require teachers to look into ways to raise the level of learning in the classroom. This change becomes challenging because many teachers believe that they are teaching at their highest level given their circumstances. The challenge of change is further extended when the task of CRP is introduced. CRP will require teachers to critically deal with the culture of the student and their cultural mismatches. The challenge of change here is two-fold. The first challenge, since 84 percent of the nation's teachers are White (Feistritzer, 2011), is changing the belief that culture does not matter to a belief system that embraces culture as a part of the learning environment. To be culturally competent means that a teacher has "the ability to successfully teach students that come from a culture other than [their] own" (Moule, 2005, p. 5). Cultural competence implies a willingness to develop interpersonal relationships, explore student culture, and create relevant learning experiences that connect to the lived cultural experiences of the student (Brown-Jeffy & Cooper, 2011; Ensign, 2003; Moule, 2005). The next challenge is adjusting instructional practices so that culture has relevancy across all content areas.

Integrating CRP with Common Core

American education has both a universal and racial/cultural problem of production. Significant percentages of students are moving through public schools unable, and potentially unwilling, to become globally competitive and socially mobile. The present routine of education, as evidenced in college enrollment data, is not preparing all students to meet the challenge of college and career readiness (U.S. Department of Education, 2012). Compounding the universal issue of American competitiveness is the issue of culture/race which results in larger disparities for African-American and Latino students who are traditionally marginalized. While CCSS will address the universal issue of raising academic rigor, there will also be a need for an integration of CRP to supply greater engagement for culturally mismatched teachers and students. In a culturally mismatched classroom, where the instructor does not culturally identify with students, the rigor of the CCSS will not be achieved without CRP. To apply focus, coherence, and rigor, three key shifts of the standards, there is an underlying assumption that the instructor believes that students are intellectually tasked for learning (CCSS, n.d.). Ladson-Billings (1995b) notes three theoretical foundations for CRP: (a) conception of self and others, (b) social relations, and (c) conceptions of knowledge. Keys to Ladson-Billings' (1995b) *conception of self and others* and *social relations* are the respective notions of teachers believing that all "students [are] capable of academic success" and demonstrating a "connectedness with all of the students" (pp. 478–480). Effective use of the CCSS requires cultural competence for globally competitive college and career readiness. Leaders will need to:

- assure that teachers are prepared through professional development to integrate both CCSS and CRP in the classroom;
- encourage experiences in teacher in-service training so that teachers can observe the necessity of exploring the conception of self and social relations in regard to cultural and linguistic development; and
- keep abreast of current professional research on multiculturalism to reference when working with teachers, students, and families of diverse backgrounds.

College- and Career-Ready in the Urban Environment

The goal of the CCSS is to produce students who are ready for college and careers in a globally competitive market. Although the standards are heavily focused on math and literacy, it has direct implications for how all content areas will be taught. Since the Common Core will include literacy standards across all disciplines, Gilles, Wang, Smith, and Johnson (2013) suggest that professional development that enables teachers to rediscover their literacy strategies within their content areas is a tool for integrating new styles of literacy into their classrooms. Beane (2013) assesses the CCSS as a combination of social efficiency, preparing students for functional roles in society, and liberal studies, a deeper exploration into the mastery of academic disciplines. As a result, a student experiencing the Common Core should emerge with the ability to meet both collegiate and labor force needs. A key focus of the standards in mathematics is to increase rigor through greater focus and coherence ("Survey Shows Strong Support for CCSS," n.d.).

Diverse students in urban settings have developmental, social, and academic needs that necessitate leadership and instruction that aligns with those demands. In urban educational environments, children and adolescents contend with teacher shortages and attrition, funding issues, low performance, and declining graduation rates (Swanson, 2009). While ethnic and socioeconomic diversity tends to predominate, urban schools are also characterized by diversity in religions, cultural mores, and languages. Research shows that youth from these backgrounds may also have challenges that hinder their social, emotional, and academic progress (Smith, Lewis, & Smith, 2012).

The CCSS were created to prepare all students, regardless of geographical locale, for the requirements of both postsecondary education and vocational paths. In this section, we will explore how the standards can be applied in urban populations that are college-bound and those that choose the workforce upon graduation.

College-Bound

While the percentage of ethnic and linguistic minorities enrolled in postsecondary institutions has been increasing for the past three decades, conversely the enrollment rates for Whites have been decreasing (Snyder & Dillow, 2013). In 2011–2012, 19 percent of Latino youth between 18 and 24 years of age were enrolled in college, at either a two- or four-year institution (Krogstad & Fry, 2014). In comparison, African American youth in the same age range had enrollment rates of 14 percent. From these data, it is clear that a noteworthy number of minority students are choosing college as a viable path after high school.

While increasing Latino and African American enrollment is lauded as progress, many of these students are matriculating without the requisite skills needed to be academically successful and persist to graduation. Research indicates that as many as 40 percent of college students need remedial work prior to enrolling in their first course, in particular those from economically disadvantaged groups (Peter D. Hart Research Associates/Public Opinion Strategies, 2005). College instructors report that students are not as prepared for the intellectually taxing work of higher education (Rothman, 2012). Since success in high school is a valid marker of achievement in college, the Common Core must provide relevant curricular content for students to gain the skills that will transfer to more advanced college-level courses.

In an effort to ensure the Common Core undergirded the requirements of postsecondary work, the developers of standard reform enlisted the expertise of representatives of the College Board and numerous college faculty and staff across the country (Rothman, 2012). The input from college professors especially highlighted the importance of reading, writing, and mathematics as predictors of success and persistence at the postsecondary level. Prior to the CCSS, literacy requirements at the high school level did not connect with the reading and writing skills essential in college (Jones & King, 2012). As an example, students who were evaluated on knowledge and comprehension-level tasks in high school were now faced with analysis and synthesis-type assignments at the collegiate level. Writing that took a more personal narrative for high school students was replaced with writing that necessitated assessment, judgment, and prediction for college students. The mathematics ability essential for students to persist at the postsecondary level involves the construction of arguments, defense of positions, and transformative problem solving as opposed to simple computation which is typical of high school math.

For urban students on a college-bound path, the Common Core provides an opportunity to practice, perfect, and receive substantive feedback on their ability to master complex tasks as first-year college students. The need for remedial education drops significantly when students work through a curriculum that requires a more advanced and deeper understanding of core concepts and ideas. College instructors, as authors and contributors to the CCSS, report that there is reliable curricular alignment between high school benchmarks and what is expected as academically prepared first-year college students. Therefore, general education leaders must assure that students in urban settings receive: (a) the same rigor as any other settings, and (b) course offerings that promote students to obtain the skills needed for matriculation to college.

Students with Mild Disabilities and At-Risk Students

Students with learning disabilities, behavioral disorders, and other mild disabilities who live in urban environments like Jamal in the vignette also have the choice of college or career paths according to their academic skill level. They are both included in general education classes and usually administered state-level assessments, some with and without accommodations. Students with disabilities will need extensive implicit instruction, and leaders will need to assure that general and special education teachers work collaboratively to ensure appropriate instruction within the confines of the Individualized Education Plan (IEP). Haager and Vaughn (2013) suggest the following strategies for students who have similar learning challenges as Jamal:

- Students may need small group instruction with guided practice within integrated lessons.

- As students with disabilities and at-risk students work in general education classes, they must receive effective tier instructions to minimize skill gaps (see Chapter 8).

- Instruction will need to be differentiated not only for skill level but to assure that students receive culturally responsive instruction (Ladson-Billings, 1995b).

- Class assignments should assure that students have multiple ways they can respond and demonstrate knowledge of the standards.

- The effective use of evidence-based methods in inclusive practices such as the *Kansas Content Enhancement Strategies* that were researched on students with learning disabilities (Lenz, Deshler, & Kissam, 2004).

Career-Bound

The CCSS were designed to provide students with the skills to thrive not only in postsecondary academic settings but also in the world of work. For urban students, academic preparation is vital, but of equal importance is the training, work-based efforts, and service learning practices students experience while in high school. As the CCSS are implemented across the country, both educators and employers are seeking to close the gap between student knowledge and industry needs. Surveys of U.S. employers highlight the discrepancy between student preparation and demonstrated ability. Almost two-fifths of employers feel high school graduates are unprepared for the demands of entry-level work in various industries (Peter D. Hart Research Associates/Public Opinion Strategies, 2005). Employers consistently lament the need for a qualified workforce, but there seems to be a small pool from which to select.

As the CCSS were a joint effort between experts, educators, and policymakers, there is a decidedly cohesive thread of preparation in academics leading to training in the workforce. The skills and abilities students demonstrate via successful completion of the Common Core curriculum underscore the needs that employers require in their employees. Strong written and verbal communication skills, problem-solving ability, advanced technology use, and critical thinking are all aptitudes industry heads need for a vibrant labor force. The standards offer students making career transitions from high school a strong knowledge base from which to launch their postsecondary paths.

The economic challenges of urban settings are well documented and most often seen in the realities of the school and public settings (Lin & Bates, 2010). Students in lower income and poor performing schools may not have access to valuable internships, career study, and technical support as others. It is imperative that school and community leaders provide opportunities for students:

- to gain work experience in the way of service learning, internships, and job corps; and
- to see direct connections between academic coursework and the requirements of their chosen career in order to incentivize high school performance.

Another critical component of school–community partnerships is the facilitation of mentoring relationships between high school students and local employers. If area industry leaders feel connected to the members of the school base, they can enable the grooming of a workforce in their own backyards. Students receive worthwhile hands-on experience, and the curriculum supports the economic and workforce needs of the area. The end result is a highly trained labor force with an investment in the betterment of the community. School leaders, within their districts and schools, should assure and encourage:

- environments that emphasize the exploration of aptitude;
- avenues of various internships through strong community connections; and
- viable means to explore technology.

Students with Severe Disabilities

Students with severe disabilities may need to follow a specified career path as their IEPs will need to be closely adhered. In many states, competencies have been outlined in the *Occupational Course of Study of Essential Skills*. Students with severe disabilities should have the opportunity to learn these standards (Courtade, Spooner, Browder, & Jimenez, 2012), but the curriculum will need to be highly adapted. Special education leaders may need to encourage:

- strong vocational support systems such as job coaching and on-the-job training; and
- hands-on experiences in the community.

School Environmental Challenges: Smoothing Rough Places

In the era of the Common Core, urban schools will be required to utilize all available resources, both human and fiscal, to ensure student success. Principals and specialists should demonstrate an understanding of how the curricular changes of the CCSS affect instruction, which subsequently affects student performance. Whereas a culture of avoiding sanctions is common in urban schools (Anagnostopoulos & Rutledge, 2007), principals should create an environment of success, accomplishment, and positivity through partnership and cooperation. Leadership must be willing to collaborate with community agencies and local constituencies in order to provide urban youth with opportunities to connect academic learning with real-world experience.

School-Based Leaders

School-based leaders in urban schools will need to address two main issues to ensure successful implementation of the CCSS: (a) novice teacher support, and (b) economic differences in the community. Urban schools have special characteristics that require a teaching skill set that comes with extensive experience (Marzano, Waters, & McNulty, 2005). To guarantee new teachers get the best chance for success early on, pairing them with a strong instructional leader will be beneficial to the development and growth of not only the teaching staff but students as well. Since urban schools are staffed with a disproportionate number of novice teachers (Billingsley, 2007), leaders in inner-city schools can address this issue by:

- providing extra support to these teachers as they make the transition to a culturally, linguistically, and economically diverse setting; and
- facilitating a mentoring relationship between veteran and novice teachers to address some of the attrition problems that occur within the first three years of teaching.

School-based leaders in urban settings also must be sensitive to the economic and cultural differences of their school community. Parents, teachers, and students coming from said environments will require a leader who has awareness and respect for those diverse backgrounds. It is not enough to have "book" knowledge about cultural and linguistically diverse populations; administrators should demonstrate:

- a commitment to advocacy, social justice, and change;
- reflective practice and relationship building; and
- a strong home–school connection whereby they reach out in various ways to disenfranchised and marginalized groups through parent advisory committees, workforce projects and town-hall meetings.

Administrators will need to begin from a position of knowledge and authority of the standards and how to best leverage their staff to meet the needs of urban students. In-service workshops, action research, professional development, and substantive feedback are ways school leadership can support teachers as they adopt the new curriculum. There should be explicit connections between the Common

Core and learning outcomes for students. School leaders will have to embrace new and different ways of supporting their staff that require unifying distinct and dissimilar voices. Collaboration will be key with consensus applied.

Special Education Leaders

The CCSS will encourage special education leaders to position themselves as advocates for the growth and development of all students, regardless of disability status. Two areas that will require closer examination include (a) implementing evidence-based practices and (b) communicating clear expectations for student success. In working with teachers and parents, special education leaders must use:

- strong research-based effective instruction and student outcomes as a guide;
- modified instructional techniques to increase achievement gains of students with disabilities (Graham & Harris, 2013; Wakeman, Karvonen, & Ahumada, 2013);
- the IEP to denote how students will progress toward the CCSS using assessment and established benchmarks; and
- technology to support the varied ways students learn and infuse Universal Design for Learning techniques (see Chapter 8).

All students, irrespective of disability status, should be encouraged to reach the heights of their abilities and potential. Leaders can support teachers by modeling respectful and inclusive language, highlighting best practices, and providing actionable feedback. A shared vision of student achievement that is cultivated from the home to the school to the larger community is imperative. Educators who work with children and youth with disabilities have important information to share that can benefit all within the school, and leadership should encourage such types of cross-instructional discussions. Special education leaders, school leaders, and teachers must work collaboratively to provide:

- a welcoming space where all students and families are valued and respected for the richness of their backgrounds;
- direction in how to implement the CCSS and link instructional strategies with key learning outcomes; and
- allocation to resources that encourage instructional excellence and student achievement.

Applying the CCSS and Solutions

Leaders have a critical role in educating and forming collaborative teams with teachers and community and families to appropriately implement CCSS in urban settings. They are the visible spokesperson who creates the opportunity to motivate collaboration. To keep a strong communication network, teamwork among district leaders is essential.

Teachers

Teachers and academic staff will require in-depth knowledge concerning teaching a diversity of students and academic levels within the classroom, as well as in-service experiences on how to adapt instructional practices to include CCSS. There is a hodgepodge of controversies related to teaching the Common Core. For urban settings, leaders will need to assure that teachers (Shanahan, 2012) do the following:

- Provide opportunities for students to link prior knowledge into assignments in order to make cultural connections; for example, it is encouraged to discuss the Civil Rights Movement or the immigration of the Latin population in a reading or social studies assignment.

- Know that the new standards do not contradict previous standards but enhance them; for example, in English classes, literature selections are not limited to just informational text but can include many more forms of language arts such as essays, journalistic readings, fiction, and the kinds of reading materials seen in the workplace.

- Use texts that are appropriate for the student grade level.

- Are consistent with the use of the standards across all types of students; every student should have the opportunity to succeed regardless of their urban community status.

- Are aware of negative and stereotypical language; rather than referring to a group of people as a disadvantaged population, use language that stresses cultural differences.

- Imbed instruction in real-life experiences; realistic activities can be easily infused into lessons because the standards have flexibility in the presentation of subjects.

- Understand the benefits of using the CCSS; for instance, CCSS are not added to the present curriculum, but infused to enhance higher order thinking skills and instructional practices and strategies.

- Understand that there are fewer topics to teach; Schmidt and Houang (2012) note that countries that have been using CCSS covered 99 topics in grades 1 through 8, whereas prior to the CCSS implementation in the United States, as many as 154 topics were presented in the same grades.

Community and Families

The Wall Street Journal in 2011 spoke of a noted trend across the United States; many families with higher incomes move away from cities where poor people are more apt to live. These families enjoy urban life and its conveniences but leave cities for better school opportunities in the suburbs. Oftentimes, these families may cluster in gated communities and other exclusive neighborhoods, while diverse populations might reside in "ethnic clusters" in the city (Kihato, Massoumi, Ruble, Subiros, & Garland, 2010). How do these types of arrangements affect school leaders and teachers when both populations attend one school? How do you accommodate all students? What does this mean for students like Jamal in the vignette? For school leaders, the interest of all groups needs to merge and connect (Michael-Luna & Marri, 2011).

School leaders want to persuade and encourage urban families to become involved in the implementation of the CCSS so they have a voice in decision making. Delguidice and Luna (2013) suggest ways that school leaders can keep urban parents informed (Chapter 4 lists other suggestions for informing parents):

- Regular, short, and informed presentations (possibly at parent–teacher meetings), tailored to the community, that include question-and-answer sessions.
- Dissemination of key facts about CCSS using social media.
- Creation of short informative films about the CCSS that can be provided on interactive sites.
- Use leaders and speakers from culturally and linguistically diverse populations within the school district to address urban audiences.

Connections to Assessment

As mentioned in Chapter 1, Partnerships for Assessment or Readiness for College Careers or Smarter Balanced Assessment Consortium are assessments created for and associated with the CCSS. There are, however, new and evolving assessments on the horizon that school leaders will need to learn (Willhoft, 2013). One such CCSS assessment that is used by urban districts is the Trial Urban District Assessment (TUDA). The scores from TUDA are reported through the National Assessment of Educational Progress, the largest national system that assesses students with a National Report Card. These scores present a more accurate measure of an urban student's progress and knowledge (Willhoft, 2013). Leaders can emphasize the use or development of:

- formative assessments, as such types of tests stress on-going growth;
- rubrics that focus on incremental growth and progress;
- summative assessments that emphasize modification of the curriculum and instructional practices;

- assessment exercises aligned to CCSS that contain critical thinking and real-world problems;

- various questioning formats that require critical thinking;

- writing and speaking assignments that focus on persuasive techniques;

- a learning community-style examination of assessment data; and

- tools that can access data, provide feedback, and share sample assessment items (McAssey, 2014; Willhoft, 2013).

Research-Based Practical Tips and Caveats

- Leaders need to be aware of the various socioeconomic statuses and cultures in the community and guarantee that no one group is ignored or uninformed when clarifying the Common Core.

- The standards were created to prepare all students for vocational or secondary paths, regardless of geographical locale (Krogstad & Fry, 2014).

- Culturally and linguistically diverse populations are choosing college as a viable path after high school at a growing rate. Therefore, it is important to prepare them for postsecondary environments.

- It is important that instructors understand cultural relevant pedagogy and infuse it into instruction in order to create a bridge from student background to new knowledge.

- *Cultural competence* means that teachers can successfully instruct students who are from a culture different than their own to create relevant learning experiences (Brown-Jeffy & Cooper, 2011; Ensign, 2003; Moule, 2005).

- Rigor and higher order thinking skills should be presented during instruction.

- The major difference between current U.S. state standards and those of leading countries is the attempt to cover too many topics (Schmidt & Houang, 2012). Leaders will need to examine and revamp the curriculum so that the CCSS is not an add-on but an integrated concept within the school system.

- Special education and general education leaders have different jobs, but collaboration is imperative when implementing the CCSS. Special education leaders must remember first and foremost that the IEP should denote how students will progress toward the CCSS, while general education leaders must remember to provide in-service professional development activities and extra support to these teachers as they make the transition to a culturally, linguistically, and economically diverse setting.

Summary

The CCSS were introduced to the United States to prepare students for success in colleges and careers and to make instruction relevant to the real world. There are cultural and racial disparities and barriers to college access and achievement. Special education and school leaders need to be aware that CCSS strategies must be specific to the economic and cultural environment. As they are implemented across the United States, leaders must collaborate, communicate, and form school–community partnerships with teachers and caregivers so that all families can understand the need for the CCSS. The main challenge for both special and general education leaders is to work with teachers to confirm they can use cultural competence within their teaching, that is, linking the school with the culture. In-service activities, research-based practices, application of data, and ongoing professional development are paramount.

Let us keep these considerations in mind as we look back at Jamal. Jamal is not your typical fifth grader—not because he lives in an urban setting and one of his parents is incarcerated in prison but because he has some skills that can carry him for lifetime of success, far more developed than most other fifth graders regardless of where they live.

But Jamal's behavior is all the school can see right now. Behavior, except in clinically diagnosed cases, is not the problem; it is the symptom. Jamal's symptoms tell us that he is at a crossroads where he can succeed in school or turn to negative choices.

Jamal understands structures of music even though he cannot formally read music. He hears them, and he can repeat them, and he can create new ones. These skills appear high on Bloom's Taxonomy. Jamal has very strong skills in in memory and problem solving. These higher order thinking skills that CCSS stresses, can be paired with music to prepare him for academic task that would increase his skill levels. Finding and using these types of interest and skill for individuals in urban communities are imperative in helping students link what they know to what they need to learn. Leaders set the stage to help teachers develop these connections.

References

Anagnostopoulos, D., & Rutledge, S. (2007, May). Making sense of school sanctioning policies in urban high schools: Charting the depth and drift of school and classroom change. *Teachers College Record, 109*, 1261–1302.

Beane, J. A. (2013). A Common Core of a different sort: Putting democracy at the center of the curriculum. *Middle School Journal, 44*(3), 6–14.

Billingsley, B. S. (2007). A case study of teacher attrition in an urban district. *Journal of Special Education Leadership, 20,* 11–20.

Brown-Jeffy, S., & Cooper, J. (2011). Toward a conceptual framework of culturally relevant pedagogy: An overview of the conceptual and theoretical literature. *Teacher Education Quarterly, 38*(1), 65–84.

Common Core State Standards initiative: Preparing America's students for college & career (2010). Retrieved from http://www.corestandards.org

Courtade, J., Spooner, F., Browder, D., & Jimenez, B. (2012). Seven reasons to promote a standards-basedinstruction for students with severe disabilities—A reply to Ayres, Lowery, Douglas, & Sievers (2011). *Education and Training in Autism and Developmental Disabilities, 47,* 3–13.

Delguidice, M., & Luna, R. (2013). Common Core—Connecting with parents. *School Library Monthly, 29*(7), 30–32.

Ensign, J. (2003). Including culturally relevant math in an urban school. *Educational Studies, 34*(4), 414–423.

Feistritzer, C. E. (2011). *Profile of teachers in the U.S. 2011.* Washington, DC: National Center for Education Information.

Garza, R. (2009). Latino and white high school students' perceptions of caring behaviors: Are we culturally responsive to our students? *Urban Education, 44,* 297. doi:10.1177/0042085908318714

Germani, G. (Ed.). (1973). *Modernization, urbanization and the urban crisis.* Boston, MA: Little, Brown & Co.

Gilles, C., Wang, Y., Smith, J., & Johnson, D. (2013) "I'm no longer just teaching history." Professional development for teaching Common Core State Standards for literacy in social studies. *Middle School Journal, 44*(3), 34–43.

Graham, S., & Harris, K. R. (2013). Common Core State Standards, writing, and students with LD: Recommendations. *Learning Disabilities Research & Practice, 28,* 28–37.

Haager, D., & Vaughn, S. (2013). The Common Core State Standards and reading: Interpretations and implications for elementary students with learning disabilities. *Learning Disabilities Research & Practice, 28*(1), 5–16.

Johnson, C. C. (2011). The road to culturally relevant science: Exploring how teachers navigate change in pedagogy. *Journal of Research in Science Teaching, 48*(2), 170–198.

Jones, A. G., & King, J. E. (2012). The Common Core State Standards. *Change, 44,* 37–43.

Kihato, C. W., Massoumi, M., Ruble, B. A., Subiros, P., & Garland, A. M. (Eds.). (2010). *Urban diversity: Space, culture, and inclusive pluralism in cities worldwide.* Baltimore, MD: Johns Hopkins University Press.

Krogstad, J. M., & Fry, R. (2014). More Hispanics, Blacks enrolling in college, but lag in bachelor's degrees. *Pew Research Center.* Retrieved from http://www.pewresearch.org/fact-tank/2014/04/24/more-hispanics-blacks-enrolling-in-college-but-lag-in-bachelors-degrees

Ladson-Billings, G. (1995a). But that's just good teaching! The case for culturally relevant pedagogy. *Theory into Practice, 34*(3), 159–165.

Ladson-Billings, G. (1995b). Toward a theory of culturally relevant pedagogy. *American Educational Research Journal, 32*(3), 465–491.

Lenz, B. K., Deshler, D. D., & Kissam, B. R. (2004). *Teaching content to all: Evidence-based inclusive practices in middle and secondary schools.* Boston, MA: Pearson.

Lin, M., & Bates, A. B. (2010). Home visits: How do they affect teachers' beliefs about teaching and diversity? *Early Childhood Education Journal, 38,* 179–185.

Marzano, R., Waters, T., & McNulty, B. (2005). *School leadership that works: From research to results*. Alexandria, VA: Association for Supervision and Curriculum Development.

McAssey, L. (2014). A Principal's View. *Principal, 93*(3), 14–18.

Michael-Luna, S., & Marri, A. (2011, January 1). Rethinking diversity in resegregated schools: Lessons from a case study of urban K–8 preservice teachers. *Urban Education, 46*(2), 178–201.

Moule, J. (2005). *Cultural competence: A primer for educators* (2nd ed.). Belmont, CA: Wadsworth.

Peter D. Hart Research Associates/Public Opinion Strategies. (2005). *Rising to the challenge: Are high school graduates prepared for college and work?* Retrieved from http://www.achieve.org/files/pollreport_0.pdf

Racial/Ethnic Enrollment in Public Schools. (2015). *National Center for Educational Statistics*. Retrieved from https://nces.ed.gov/programs/coe/indicator_cge.asp

Rothman, R. (2012). A Common Core of readiness. *Educational Leadership, 69*, 10–15.

Schmidt, W. H., & Houang, R. T. (2012). Curricular coherence and the Common Core State Standards for mathematics. *Educational Researcher, 41*(8), 294–308.

Shanahan, T. (2012, December 1). The Common Core ate my baby and other urban legends. *Educational Leadership, 70*(4), 10–16.

Smith, D., Lewis, C., & Smith, L. (2012). Increasing the academic success of urban schools: An examination of successful teachers. *National Journal of Urban Education & Practice, 6*(2), 115–129.

Snyder, T. D., & Dillow, S. A. (2013). *Digest of education statistics 2012* (NCES 2014-015). Washington, DC: National Center for Education Statistics, Institute of Education Sciences, U.S. Department of Education.

State and County Estimates for 1995. (1995). *United States Census Bureau*. Retrieved from http://www.census.gov/did/www/saipe/data/statecounty/data/1995.html

Survey Shows Strong Support for CCSS. (n.d.). *Achieve*. Retrieved from http://www.achieve.org/survey-shows-strong-support-ccss

Swanson, C. B. (2009). *Closing the graduation gap: Educational and economic conditions in America's largest cities*. Bethesda, MD: Editorial Projects in Education, Inc.

U.S. Department of Commerce, Economics and Statistics Administration. (2003). *2000 census of population and housing*. Washington, DC: United States Census Bureau.

U.S. Department of Education. (2012). *The condition of education: Immediate transition to college* (Indicator 34). Washington, DC: National Center for Education Statistics, Institute of Education Sciences, U.S. Department of Education. Retrieved from http://nces.ed.gov/programs/coe/pdf/coe_trc.pdf

Wakeman, S., Karvonen, M., & Ahumada, A. (2013). Changing instruction to increase achievement for students with moderate to severe intellectual disabilities. *Teaching Exceptional Children, 46*, 6–13.

Willhoft, J. (2013). Assessing progress toward college and career readiness. *Principal, 92*(4), 26–29.

Wirth, L. (1938). Urbanism as a way of life. *American Journal of Sociology, 44*(1), 1–24.

CHAPTER

7

Children with Disabilities and Those At Risk

Irene Meier, Nicole Conners, and Gloria D. Campbell-Whatley

Denise, a ninth-grade student, was identified as having a learning disability in reading. Recently, she moved to an urban school in the northern United States in a major large city. She was identified in middle school and has been served in inclusive settings. She seemingly made an effort in middle school to perform academic task, but now she never completes homework, does not participate in any extracurricular activities and is failing all of her classes. She is late to school and class, inattentive, and defiant. She comes from a single-parent home and her mother has a job working in the evening. Her father is not in her life. She frequently has other young people her age at her house in the evenings, and it does not appear that they are studying. How do we adapt the CCSS for Denise?

Introduction

Students with disabilities are going to be challenged to excel within the general curriculum and be prepared for success in their post-school lives; this includes college and/or careers. According to Individuals with Disabilities Education Act (IDEA), each student with a disability has Individualized Education Plan (IEP), and educational planning is determined on an individual basis. The standards are rigorous, yet students with disabilities my not be able to match that rigor. This chapter will outline the infusion of the Common Core standards into the educational plans of the students with disabilities, students under 504, and students at risk (i.e., poverty, free and reduced lunch) and the services and accommodations to support them.

A Balancing Act

Since the inception of No Child Left Behind (NCLB) in 2002, the balancing act of meeting educational accountability for all children across the nation began. It initially began as a call for accountability that all students in various subgroups, including those with disabilities, would reach academic proficiency by the year 2014 (NCLB, 2002). While 2014 seemed to be a long way off, there were sanctions to be imposed if districts did not meet their specific state targets by 2014. Even though NCLB was a reauthorization of the Elementary and Secondary School Act focused on Title I practice initially, it soon had far-reaching implications into non-Title I school sites across the U.S. school districts.

Originally, attorneys challenged NCLB and believed the law to be unconstitutional, one citing this federal legislation as crossing the line into state jurisdiction over education policy (McColl, 2005). The individual states all responded in their own unique ways to this federal call for accountability causing disparity and inequity in public education across the nation. The balancing act began first with assessment leaders at the state level trying to determine adequate summative tests in the four core subjects required by NCLB of reading, math, science, and social studies. Many states did not have common assessments in place for these core subjects, and several states did not have statewide standards. Assessment practices began to drive the instruction in the absence of content-level standards.

Another balancing act occurred when states attempted to set an n size for the various subgroups required to have individualized test performance reports. The n size refers to the minimum number of students required to take a state assessment in order for that subgroup to be counted for a given school or school district. Some states like South Carolina and Tennessee, for example, used a variety of n sizes for the different subgroups, while states like North Carolina held the n size stable across all subgroups. States with higher n sizes for the subgroups that were showing more difficulty began to show some success. However, it was not necessarily due to their educational practices but due to a higher n size for a particular group. The disparity began to widen among states with respect to how each was measuring the achievement of students in the various subgroups.

It was soon discovered that districts had varying practices in terms of their accountability measures, the number of students actually counted in a given subgroup, their paraprofessional and teacher credentialing to meet the highly qualified standards, and most importantly their curriculum standards. The curriculum standards became an issue because it was clear that it would be difficult to hold a nation accountable for student achievement when the states were so disparate in meeting the requirements of NCLB. It was clear that some consistency was required. It happened first with standardizing the n across the nation so that all subgroups were at the same level (40) and the next step was to make uniform standards so that regardless of what state a child lived in, the same equitable standards would be in force. Hence, the formation of the CCSS is to bring unity in curriculum and rigor across standards throughout the United States.

While that may have seemed like a rather obvious and simple solution to the inconsistent implementation of NCLB across the nation, the various policy groups that advocated for CCSS created even more balancing acts that school districts across the nation continue to face. While it was initially thought to be very important that all states have common standards and maintain a certain level of rigor, it soon became apparent that implementation with fidelity was going to become a huge issue. Each state interpreted and implemented the CCSS through their own lens. Moats (2012) encouraged the CCSS be viewed for its strengths and weaknesses and interpreted with reference to research we know about teaching students with disabilities.

What we do know about teaching students with disabilities is that districts must be committed to facilitating student access to the general education curriculum (Cortiella & Burnette, 2009; Telfer, 2012). The CCSS does provide targeted focus on skills that students need to progress from grade to grade and to graduate successfully. The CCSS also provides information to parents as to what is required for students with disabilities to be college- and career-ready upon graduation (Thurlow, 2013). Some of challenges that students with disabilities face are low expectations (Jorgensen, 2005) and the inability to access the general curriculum (Thurlow, 2012). Special educators have faced challenges receiving professional development on the general curriculum standards (Bolt & Roach, 2009; Laitusis & Cook, 2007).

Another concern is that IEPs are not being consistently implemented throughout districts and states (Thurlow, 2013). Standards-based IEPs are required by federal regulation for those students who are accessing an alternate assessment based on modified achievement standards (AA-MAS). Given the NCLB waiver status of many states, the AA-MAS are disappearing since states are not permitted to use this form of assessment under the waiver. As a result, standards-based IEPs have been decreasing. The following sections will explore the use of CCSS with students who have mild to severe disabilities, those who are eligible for 504 accommodations and services, and the challenges that school and division leadership face with implementation.

Students with Mild Disabilities

The balancing act for students with mild or high-incidence disabilities such as those with specific learning disabilities, emotional disabilities, and some health impairments can be quite challenging. Many of these students are accessing general education classes on a full-time basis and experience the rigor of the changes in the standards in many states. Approximately 85 percent of students with disabilities may have difficulties learning due to their disability, but this does not prevent them from learning with the same state standards as other students (Camara & Quenemoen, 2012; Thurlow, 2010). While most students with disabilities receive their education in general education classes, this does not mean that all states and school divisions are providing equal access to the curriculum based on the state standards (Nolet & McLaughlin, 2005). The same applies to the curriculum now based on Common Core standards in many states.

What may be new for elementary teachers (K–5) regarding CCSS is the focus on critical literacy skills required to prepare students for college and career readiness. They target reading across texts and genres, increasing in complexity as the grades progress. The elementary focus is on preparing students in reading, writing, listening, and speaking, including deep analysis and close reading (Haager & Vaughn, 2013). The majority of students identified under IDEA eligibility across the nation have a specific learning disability primarily in reading. The increased rigor of the literacy CCSS certainly poses challenges to students with specific learning disabilities. Supports will be needed in providing foundational literacy skills to students with specific learning disabilities so they may access reading across varying content. Also, accommodations in the general education classroom will be required so that students can continue to access this curriculum (Haager & Vaughn, 2013).

Haager and Vaughn (2013) provide suggestions for both special and general education elementary teachers to assist students with learning disabilities (K–5) achieve success with CCSS. Students like Denise will really need the modification listed next. Special education teachers should do the following:

- Develop an in-depth understanding of the components of the CCSS and how they can be adjusted for students with learning disabilities.
- Work collaboratively with general educators to develop a plan for instruction.
- Practice integrated literacy lessons across content so that students can access general education classes successfully.

General education teachers should do the following:

- Continue effective practices in Tier 1 and 2 instruction aimed to improve reading foundational skills.
- Provide appropriate instruction to minimize students being referred to special education.
- Collectively work with others to plan and implement differentiated instruction.
- Collaborate specifically with special education and support staff.
- Afford students multiple response methods to demonstrate their knowledge.
- Provide students a range of reading passages that they can read successfully.

The CCSS in literacy for history and social studies present many challenges for adolescents with specific learning disabilities as students are challenged to engage in higher order thinking and reasoning skills (Bulgren, Graner, & Deshler, 2013). Brownell, Mellard, and Deshler (1993) have noted that adolescents with specific learning disabilities have difficulty mastering these skills. Students often lack the skills related to organizing and processing information, making inferences, and distinguishing the details from the main idea (DiCecco & Gleason, 2002). Due to the higher level demands across content areas and the difficulties documented for adolescents with learning disabilities, the curriculum challenges in middle and high school become greater (Swanson & Deshler, 2003). While there are challenges with CCSS for students with disabilities in literacy for history and social studies, there are often opportunities.

Suggested recommendations on instructional practices, supports, and services designed to accommodate students with learning disabilities have been included in CCSS. Thus, the needs of students with learning disabilities are recognized in CCSS and they reinforce the goals of IDEA (2004) in terms of providing modifications and accommodations so students with disabilities can experience success in the general education classroom (Bulgren et al., 2013). Universal Design for Learning (UDL) offers students supports by providing multiple means of representation, action, expression, and engagement (CAST, 2011). Additional instructional supports in explicit instruction in strategies, use of a comprehensive reading program, instructional accommodations, and assistive technology services are also outlined and demonstrate that the needs of students with learning disabilities are being recognized in CCSS (Bulgren et al., 2013). Strategies like these would be helpful for Denise in the vignette.

Challenges certainly exist for both general and special education teachers to meet the diverse needs of students with mild disabilities, including those with specific learning disabilities. While not all teachers may be willing to make the instructional adjustments necessary (Deshler, Deshler, & Biancarosa, 2007), supports will need to be provided in terms of professional development and instructional coaching so that teachers can make both technical and adaptive changes they will need to make (Bulgren et al., 2013; Heifetz & Linsky, 2002). Technical change is described as acquiring new knowledge to perform a teaching role in a different way. Adaptive change involves teachers changing their belief structure relative to expectations and attitudes toward teaching. Multiple opportunities should be provided so teachers can learn new skills and collaborate with other colleagues.

Students with disabilities who experience mathematics disabilities may also have difficulty accessing CCSS. The overlap with CCSS in mathematics and existing state standards is judged to be only 20–35 percent (Porter, McMaken, Hwang, & Yang, 2011). The CCSS differed in that it emphasized conceptual understanding over memorization (Porter et al., 2011). However, when a state adopts CCSS in mathematics, they can expect to experience changes that come with adopting a new curriculum such as changes in teaching practices which lead to changes in professional development (Cobb & Jackson, 2011). In some states, standards are aligned with the *Principles and Standards for School Mathematics* (2000) introduced by the National Council of Teachers of Mathematics (NCTM). The CCSS outlines specific skills to be taught at each grade level, while the NCTM standards emphasize skills at grade bands and do not include as many skills. For example, the CCSS lists 14 standards for fourth grade, while the NCTM lists four expectations for grades 3–5 (Powell, Fuchs, & Fuchs, 2013).

Students with Severe Disabilities

The balancing act for students with severe or low-incidence disabilities such as autism, multiple disabilities, intellectual disabilities, and sensory disabilities becomes one of access and professional development so that instructors have the correct skills and methodology to teach this unique population of students (Courtade, Spooner, Browder, & Jimenez, 2012). Approximately 15 percent or less of students with disabilities have significant cognitive disabilities. These students should be held to the same content standards as other students but different achievement standards (Kleinert, Kearns, Quenemoen, & Thurlow, 2013; Quenemoen, 2008). We must ensure that students with severe disabilities are accessing the CCSS through the aligned standards, UDL, appropriate individualized technology, and standards-based IEPs. We must also ensure that students with moderate to severe disabilities will leave school with a meaningful transition to postsecondary programs or to employment (Carter et al., 2010). College and career readiness training has been expanded throughout the nation to include students with disabilities and now even those with severe disabilities.

According to Wakeman, Karvonen, and Ahumada (2013), teachers must be able to change instruction to meet the needs of students with moderate to severe disabilities who are accessing the Common Core standards. Since the reauthorization of IDEA in 1997, access to academic content has been required for students with significant cognitive disabilities. Upon reauthorization of IDEA in 2004, access and "progress" in the general education curriculum became a requirement. Since 2001, teachers of students with significant disabilities have been required to utilize alternate assessments to demonstrate progress. Through the need for alternate assessment, many teachers learned how to change their instruction so that their students could demonstrate progress on a subset of alternate state standards that were aligned to the state curriculum standards. The Common Core standards posed many new challenges for this population of students in particular as well as for the teachers required to meet these standards.

Ways to meet the challenging demands of the Common Core standards for students with significant disabilities can be discussed by changes in (Wakeman et al.,

2013) (a) instruction, (b) content, and (c) student performance. Results of research studies show that changes in instruction can occur through:

- The use of task analysis which has been documented throughout the literature as an effective methodology for teaching academic content to students with disabilities by utilizing forward and backward chaining (Spooner, Browder, & Mims, 2011), instruction in math (Browder, Jimenez, & Trela, 2012), and scientific inquiry (Courtade, Browder, & Spooner, 2010).

- The use of systematic instruction in literacy instruction (Browder, Ahlgrim-Delzell, Spooner, & Baker, 2009).

- Reductions in the complexity of content presented to students can also improve student performance. Complexity can be increased or decreased through a number of manipulatives present in a math lesson (Browder, Spooner, Ahlgrim-Delzell, Wakeman, & Harris, 2008) or by changing the number of tasks in a task analysis (Spooner et al., 2011).

- Changing the abstractness of the objects/symbols presented may also be needed. Research indicates that many students with significant cognitive disabilities rely on concrete symbols such as objects progressing to use of text (Towles-Reeves, Kearns, Kleinert, & Kleinert, 2009), while instruction should be designed to facilitate symbolic language as appropriate (Browder, Ahlgrim-Delzell, Courtade-Little, & Snell, 2006).

- The use of technology is also well documented in the literature as an instructional aid for this population of students (Ayres, Maguire, & McClimon, 2009).

Students with significant cognitive disabilities may respond to instruction in a variety of ways through:

- nonverbal or verbal communication, using low-tech or high-tech systems;
- the use of concrete symbols or text;
- varying the complexity of response and matching the correct response;
- the use of graphic organizers that can improve student responses (Wakeman et al., 2013); and
- teacher prompting can affect the accuracy of student responses; by varying the hierarchy of prompting (least to most or most to least intrusive prompts) (Spooner et al., 2011).

In summary, the Common Core standards designed for all students, including those with significant disabilities, have caused teachers to redefine their instruction and expectations for students. They will need to vary their instructional techniques to utilize evidence-based components of systematic instruction such as chaining and task analysis (Spooner et al., 2011), vary the content presented, as well as the response levels expected from students. Using UDL (discussed more in-depth later and in Chapter 8) to enhance instruction and response mode will be critically important.

The Common Core Standards and Students Eligible for Section 504

Section 504 of the Rehabilitation Act (1973) is legislation designed to eliminate discrimination on the basis of disability in any program receiving federal funding. Section 504 guarantees access to full participation and a free and appropriate public education (FAPE) to all children regardless of the nature or severity of their disability. Students who are eligible under Section 504 (1973) have a right to access the Common Core standards with accommodations. Specific accommodations, modifications, and, in some instances, special education or related services under the auspices of FAPE must be provided to eligible students to ensure this access. The 2008 amendments reemphasize the need for students eligible for 504 plans to receive a FAPE. The distinction between the provision of FAPE in IDEA (2004) and Section 504 (1973) has not been fully defined.

In order to qualify for a *504* plan under this provision, a student must (Section 504 of Rehabilitation Act, 1973):

- have a physical or mental impairment that substantially limits one or more major life activities;
- have a record of such an impairment; and
- be regarded as having such an impairment.

Once a student qualifies, a *504* plan is drafted by parents and school staff focused on providing accommodations, supports, and services to eligible students. With the inception of the Common Core standards, the rigor of state standards has increased in many cases, thereby making it more difficult for students with a disability under *504* to achieve success. As the rigor of the curriculum increases across the nation, the request for *504* plans will potentially increase because many students not identified under IDEA (2004) who still present with a disability will need assistance in order to achieve success. In addition to services and classroom accommodations under Section 504 (1973), testing accommodations will also be required. In some states these students will qualify for alternate types of assessment. States will need to define this unique and growing population of students as they develop alternate assessments relative to the Common Core standards. The increase in student plans, accommodations, and alternate testing will also affect the work load on the counselors, administrators, school psychologists, and administrators tasked with attending *504* meetings and implementing these plans.

The Common Core Standards and the IEP

Careful analysis of the standards and linking the essential knowledge, skills, and understandings within each of the standards to develop IEP goals for students with disabilities is crucial work at the beginning of this initiative (McLaughlin, 2012). This process is called *deconstruction* which means that the standards are divided into small, explicit learning targets which is essential for developing annual IEPs and when planning lessons, units, and assessments (Deconstruct Standards to Align IEP Goals with Common Core, 2014). Knowledge, reasoning, skill, and product targets must be examined intensely. Thoughtful thinking around the knowledge, skills, and understandings of each standard is necessary and an understanding of how the standards align with individualized IEP goals is essential to ensure that students with disabilities are successful learners within the core standards.

At-Risk Learners

All diverse learners display a wide array of strengths, needs, skills, interests, and background experiences. Today's schools must address the growing needs of these diverse students. Yet, the current educational workforce does not represent the expanding student diversity present in today's schools. According to the National Center for Education Statistics, in 2011–2012 school year, 82 percent of 3.4 million public school teachers were non-Hispanic white, while 7 percent were non-Hispanic black and 8 percent were Hispanic. Today's teachers are not representative of the populations they serve. Consequently many educators do not have backgrounds or experiences to meet the needs of diverse students. Many of today's educators are ill-equipped through their college preparation programs and previous teaching experiences to apply aspects of cultural competence to meet the needs of culturally diverse students (Maxwell, 2014).

Students with disabilities in particular require flexible, supportive teachers who provide instructional accommodations to support access to the curriculum. Many of these diverse students, including students with disabilities, have been marginalized in their school experiences by attending schools which lack adequate school resources, highly qualified teachers, and consistently demonstrate lower student achievement (Olson & Land, 2007). This contributes greatly to the difficulties that diverse student populations have in finding success in school and preparing them for the future (discussed in more detail in Chapter 6).

Today's educational workforce, both administrators and practitioners, must address widening achievement gaps and be accountable for transforming low performing schools to adequately meet the varied needs of all students. This will require teachers with strong efficacy to hold the belief that they have the skills and knowledge to teach any student who walks into their classroom. These master teachers would need to be skilled in engaging students in real-life applications and linking to students' background knowledge.

Measurable achievement gaps for at-risk groups of students in math and English have created an urgent need to engage in systematic school improvement to increase achievement outcomes for all students. CCSS are an effort to standardize a set of educational standards and provide consistent learning goals for English language arts and mathematics. Common Core academic standards set the bar high for every learner and were developed to ensure all students graduate from high school with skills and knowledge to succeed in college, career, and life ("About the Standards," n.d.).

Methodologies for At-Risk Populations

Our nation's schools are at a historic crossroads. The implementation of the Common Core standards is a unique opportunity to set high expectations for all students with rigorous instructional content and higher order thinking. Yet, today's reality in public schools is that some students will require much more support and intervention in order to be successful learners. Strategic and purposeful thinking around the merging of systems and processes such as UDL, Response to Intervention (RTI), and high-quality teaching, with a focus on increased student engagement around the Common Core standards, is essential to ensure that all students graduate with the skills necessary to prepare for college and career.

UDL (discussed further in Chapter 8) is an evidence-based framework for curriculum design that explores teaching methods, materials, and assessments that enable all learners to be successful. This framework based on neuroscience helps to reduce barriers that are fundamentally present in rigorous learning. UDL is based on three principles: (a) learners access and acquire information in different ways, (b) learners express what they know in different ways, and (c) learners require "different types of engagement" to sustain attention and increase motivation and excitement about learning (see Chapter 8) (CAST, 2011).

CCSS promotes a culture of high expectations for all students, including those from culturally diverse backgrounds and for students with disabilities. Applying instructional supports from the three principles of UDL can help promote learning for all. Technology use is a large part of UDL. The use of assistive technology devices and services for students with disabilities in particular (IDEA, 2004c) within the UDL framework will help to ensure that all students are able to not only access the general education but also demonstrate successful learning.

UDL is closely connected to RTI or a Multi-tiered System of Supports (MTSS) (see Figure 7.1) which is designed to enable schools to provide appropriate levels of instruction and intervention based on individual needs.

RTI/MTSS are a leveled system which addresses both behavior and academic needs of students. This evidenced-based, tiered decision-making process supports implementation of high-quality core instruction for all and provides varying levels of intervention to improve learning outcomes for all students. Tier 1 or core universal instruction outlines the components of quality instruction and supports within general education curriculum (Gamm et al., 2012). The assumption is that core instruction is evidence-based, rigorous, and aligned to the Common Core standards. High-quality core instruction for all requires differentiated practices to meet varied student needs through thoughtful planning and lesson design. Optimal learning for all requires differentiation through whole group, small group, and individual supports and the use of instructional scaffolds and strategies to build a bridge from student to high-level task (Sousa & Tomlinson, 2011). Extensive knowledge of learner profiles and building meaningful student relationships are necessary components in a differentiated classroom. Proactive and purposeful planning for differentiation should be connected explicitly to the three main principles outlined in the UDL framework to ensure that accommodations and supports within the curriculum are implemented with veracity for all students.

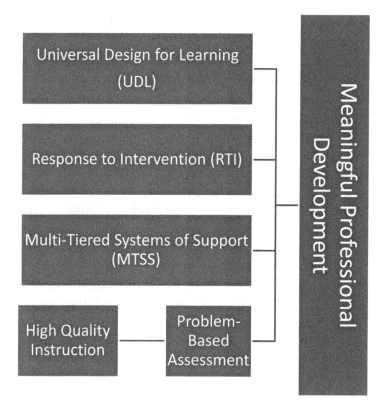

Figure 7.1 UDL Conceptual Framework and Connections

Tier 2 supports necessitate more focused, targeted instruction for some students who share common academic or behavioral needs. Tier 3 provides intensive and individualized supports for a few students based on individual needs. The supports in Tier 2 and 3 are in addition to core instruction for all and do not remove students from accessing rigorous, aligned core standards. All decision making within the tiered supports is based on data and progress monitoring to ensure that the interventions provided are aligned to student need and core standards (Gamm et al., 2012).

Professional Development

The effectiveness of the implementation of the Common Core standards for ideal learning for all students is contingent upon the development and delivery of meaningful, embedded professional development for today's educators. Given that most teachers do not have educational backgrounds and experiences that match the population they serve creates a need for meaningful professional development, not only around the core standards themselves but, more importantly, with an intense focus on supporting teachers in meeting the needs of all learners, including students with disabilities. This is a crucial consideration of any professional development and must be delivered differently since 90 percent of teachers who have participated in workshop-style training sessions rate them as ineffective in changing teacher practices (Darling-Hammond & Adamson, 2010). The successful implementation of the CCSS is contingent upon the delivery of job-embedded professional development. Schools which implement CCSS in haste without enough training usually are unsuccessful at raising student scores (Catch "Gap Students" During Transition to Common Core, 2014).

Meaningful professional development must address the need for sustained changes in educator practice. Professional development needs to be supported through collaborative processes where teachers learn from each other within professional learning communities (PLCs) (examples in Chapter 9) and share their expertise with colleagues to benefit overall student learning. Gulamhussein (2013) proposes a need for effective professional development in an era of high-stakes accountability that is ongoing and carried out over time, throughout the school year. Job-embedded professional development, related to a teacher's subject area, with an opportunity for peer and mentor support through modeling, collaboration, and coaching, is the only way to implement professional development with fidelity and to sustain changes in practice.

All teachers must be provided ongoing job-embedded professional development to develop a "pedagogy of plenty," or high-quality teaching, to reach all students. Providing a "pedagogy of plenty" or just good teaching includes strategies such as authentic learning tasks, active learning, student dialogue, inquiry-based learning, problem-based learning tasks, and peer collaboration for problem solving. It is the incorporation of these evidence-based research strategies and instructional scaffolds that are woven into the CCSS that will help to support learning while engaging students in rigorous tasks that are relevant and respectful to all backgrounds (Cole, 2008).

A Parent's Perspective

Regardless of a child's needs in special education, the adaptation to CCSS will require adjustments for parents. Parents will need to work with school leaders to be sure that their child leaves school college- or career-ready. The IEP is the center of the academic plan for each student with disabilities. Parents will need in-put to assure that standards-based IEPs meet the instructional needs of their child. For now, this will most likely be a learning process between parents and teachers that will hopefully be supported by administrators. Parents must be advocates to assure that the "special" remains in special education and services are adapted and modified appropriately (Samuels, 2011).

Of course, each goal on the student's IEP is not going to be aligned with the standards, especially those with severe disabilities. Many students will still need functional skills, even though they may participate at some skill level commensurate with students in general education (Courtade-Little & Browder, 2005).

Parents will need to work proactively with teachers as it relates to literacy requirements because reading requirements may increase. According to the CCSS, text will be more complex and higher order thinking strategies will be used. Teachers and parents will need to work collectively to rethink the strategies used with students with disabilities. Materials and methods for students with disabilities will need to be chosen more carefully. Districts will need to quickly move from explaining the CCSS with parents of children with disabilities to showing parents what these lessons and skills will look like in actual instruction in the classroom. Parents will need to see how these skills align with the IEP and the impact on students with disabilities (Dolman, 2013; Schaffhauser, 2013).

School Environmental Challenges and Solutions: Smoothing Rough Places

There will be challenges for both school and special education leaders. Solutions for each group are delineated.

School-Based Leaders

There is no doubt that challenges are great for those building-level administrators who must ensure a FAPE in a child's least restrictive environment (LRE) using evidence-based practices and employing highly qualified teachers and paraprofessionals under IDEA (2004a) and NCLB (2002). Adding accessing the CCSS and making progress on state performance examinations to the requirements will be a reason for principals to need assistance with special education services in their buildings.

McLaughlin (2012) gives good insight for elementary principals who are implementing CCSS. She recommends that:

- Principals consider the unique needs of students with disabilities and provide appropriate individual programming for them. Providing appropriate accommodations and modifications that assist students with disabilities in accessing the core standards is also key.
- Principals hire quality special educators who use evidence-based practices such as direct, explicit instruction and frequent progress monitoring.

According to Johnson, Berg, and Donaldson (2005), teaching is most important to in-school influence on student learning and it is critical that principals hire quality special educators who can effectively teach students with disabilities. However, recruiting highly qualified special educators has become increasingly more difficult.

Special Education Leaders

District-level special education leaders must understand the core standards and how they impact students with disabilities in terms of access, standards-based IEPs, alternate assessment, and UDL. Special education leaders must know that:

- Professional development must be provided to building-level administrators, district administrators, teachers, and paraprofessionals regarding accessing CCSS in the LRE using evidence-based practices.
- The use of webinars and other online systems of professional development has become a popular way of dissemination of information and training to school personnel.

Until special education becomes more than a "place" and becomes a viable support service in many districts, it will be difficult for students with disabilities to fully access the CCSS. This requires a paradigm shift from both general education and special education building and central office leaders. Leaders will need to recognize that:

- To effectively educate all students. The two disciplines of general and special education need to be interconnected and highly collaborative rather than continuing to educate students with disabilities in separate settings.

- Professional development needs to be provided to all teachers. Until we embrace one system instead of parallel systems, we will not be able to ensure the success of students with disabilities while implementing CCSS.

Applying the Common Core Standards and Solutions

The demographics within the United States have been changing rapidly over the last two decades. Subsequently, K–12 schools across the nation are experiencing an increased influx in the enrollment of culturally and linguistically diverse students, students of color, and economically disadvantaged students. For the first time the number of non-Hispanic white students will be surpassed by the combined numbers of Hispanic, Asian, and African American students. This new collective student majority, projected to be 50.3 percent by the National Center for Education Statistics, is due to the tremendous growth within the Latino population specifically and a gradual decline in the white population (Maxwell, 2014). An even bigger shift is the rise in the number of students who do not speak English as their first language. "By 2050, 34% of U.S. children younger than 17 will be immigrants themselves or the children of at least one parent who is an immigrant based on projections from the Pew Research Center" (Maxwell, 2014, p. 15). Concentrated thinking on how to meet the needs of the growing number of culturally diverse students is crucial with the implementation of the Common Core standards (see Chapter 6).

Students with disabilities are another group that will be greatly impacted by the Common Core standards due to their disability characteristics that impact not only access (IDEA, 2004) but also progress within the general education curriculum. The number of children and youth, aged 3–21, receiving special education services was 6.4 million in 2011–2012, or about 13 percent of all public school students. Students with learning disabilities are the most prevalent disability and represent 36 percent of the population (U.S. Department of Education & National Center for Education Statistics, 2014). Most of these students are accessing the curriculum with their age-level peers in general education settings for a majority of their day. The Common Core offers a notable opportunity for students with disabilities to access rigorous academic standards, yet such an undertaking cannot occur without thoughtful consideration around the distinctive needs of students with disabilities. In-depth reflection of how the rigorous Common Core standards are taught and assessed for students with disabilities is vital. McLaughlin (2012) applies key principles for providing access to the core standards:

- Recognizing that students with disabilities are a heterogeneous group who require IEP.

- The use of specific interventions such as explicit, intensive instruction and frequent monitoring of student achievement as crucial components of any instruction for students with disabilities.

- The schoolwide assessment process which measures growth and progress for all students, in addition to end-of-year assessments mandated by the Common Core standards is recommended.

Connections to Assessments

CCSS and the assessment of student learning are deeply interconnected. Student learning is no longer about the regurgitation of facts and knowledge on an end-of-course multiple choice assessment. NCLB established a need for school accountability, but it narrowed the curriculum significantly for all students, especially those from diverse backgrounds and students with disabilities. NCLB encouraged teachers to focus on a limited scope of content which addressed specific standards and indicators through multiple choice assessments. A focus on teaching to the test and emphasizing discrete indicators or benchmarks within a state's standards are all too commonplace in today's classrooms. The highest priority for learning within CCSS is how students apply knowledge and thinking, not just the recall of discrete facts that are quickly forgotten on multiple choice tests (Darling-Hammond & Adamson, 2010).

The CCSS promotes teaching all students to think and apply big understandings in order to make connections and problem-solve. This requires thoughtful thinking around how to measure student learning effectively. Reflective teachers use formative assessments on a daily basis to modify their instruction and to make changes as dictated by learner needs. These informal assessment practices must be a part of a differentiated, responsive classroom. Yet, as school districts grapple with the development of instructional materials and curriculum around the Common Core standards, they must also connect instructional materials to the development of problem-based measures that allow all students to demonstrate what they know in varied ways. New assessments have been created around the Common Core to allow students to craft their own responses and to demonstrate the depth and breadth of their knowledge and understandings within high-level tasks.

Performance assessments can measure students' cognitive thinking and reasoning skills and the ability to craft their responses in real-world applications (Darling-Hammond & Adamson, 2010). Providing teachers with the knowledge and understanding of how to develop and use performance-based assessments will be challenging. Meaningful professional development for educators around the creation of problem-based learning and performance assessments related to high-level tasks are crucial components in the beginning stages of the development of effective assessments.

Practical Tips and Caveats

- Districts must be committed to facilitating student access to the general curriculum (Cortiella & Burnette, 2009; Telfer, 2012). Low expectations set for students with disabilities and their inability to access the general curriculum is just one of the challenges. Both general and special educators need professional development to correct this problem (Bolt & Roach, 2009; Laitusis & Cook, 2007; Thurlow, 2012).

- IEPs need to be appropriately aligned and implemented consistently throughout districts and states (Thurlow, 2013). Specific accommodations and modifications must be provided to ensure student access.

- With CCSS, changes in teaching practices will lead to changes in professional development (Cobb & Jackson, 2011). Workshop-style practices were rated as ineffective for changing teacher instruction (Darling-Hammond & Adamson, 2010). Meaningful professional development through PLCs (forms in Chapter 9) with teachers learning from each other in job-embedded situations is most successful

- Alternative assessments will need to be developed for special populations and teachers will need to know how to create them (Wakeman et al., 2013). Performance-based measures that assess cognitive skills that are applicable to real-world applications is what will be needed.

- UDL and multi-tiered systems will need to be incorporated into the schools' instruction as they reduce barriers for learning for students with disabilities and at-risk youngsters. Teachers will need to be prepared to address students from all cultures. Proactive planning for differentiation is paramount.

- We must ensure that students with severe disabilities are accessing the CCSS through the aligned standards, UDL, appropriate individualized technology, and standards-based IEPs. We must also ensure that students will leave school with a meaningful transition to postsecondary programs for students with moderate to severe disabilities or to employment (Carter et al., 2010).

Summary

The CCSS brings an opportunity for public schools to set high expectations for all students around rigorous standards. The challenge for many public school educators and administrators is the paradigm shift in thinking about rigorous learning for all students. Today's educators are expected to prepare diverse students for college and career by allowing for more self-directed learning through the use of technology. Educators must build a sense of belonging and a strong classroom culture built on deeper relationships with every child and family. All educators must differentiate and provide instructional scaffolds within their instruction and assessment to ensure success for every student. They must be thoughtful and observant practitioners who are flexible and can problem-solve when supporting all students. They are, in reality, action researchers within their own classroom practice.

Yet, the success of the CCSS in maximizing learning for all students is not just about designing high-quality curriculum and performance-based assessments, but measureable success within this initiative hinges on other factors too. There must be an emphasis placed on the development of collective responsibility across individual schools and all teachers while implementing the CCSS. Stoll, Bolam, McMahon, Wallace, and Thomas (2006) consider collective responsibility an essential characteristic within a school community which creates a united belief that all teachers work to do their best to advance all students' learning. These scholars also concluded that "collective responsibility helps to sustain commitment, puts peer pressure and accountability on those who do not do their fair share, and eases isolation" (Stoll et al., 2006, p. 8). Failure to meet the expectations for higher level learning for all is conceivable without the intentional development of collective responsibility around student learning,

In addition, administrators must approach teacher learning in a similar fashion to student learning. An administrator's ability to maximize impact on student achievement must include a focus on developing teacher efficacy across every classroom and teacher within a school. It is inevitable that some teachers will need more support than others in building skills and teacher efficacy. Tschannen-Moran and Hoy (2001) identify the impact of teacher efficacy on educational outcomes such as teachers' persistence, enthusiasm, commitment and instructional behavior, as well as how students view themselves as learners in regard to their achievement, motivation, and self-efficacy beliefs. Teachers with robust teacher efficacy believe that they have the skills to teach all students and that every student will learn. These highly effective educators work tirelessly to improve the educational outcomes for all students. A necessary component in schools today is to allow time for teachers to collaborate and learn from each other. This collective work is centrally important to establish a strong cohesive school culture and individual teacher efficacy across teams and grade levels within a school.

The last essential factor, but one of equal importance, is the development of a growth mindset when thinking about students and how they learn, especially for students like Denise. Accepting students where they are and building bridges from students to higher level learning tasks is crucial work around the CCSS.

Denise's real-world urban experiences will need to be part of the classroom experiences. All students learn differently and have unique learning profiles (Sousa & Tomlinson, 2011). What kinds of things peak her interest. Has her interest changed since middle school? Students exhibit specific strengths and challenges within their learner profiles. To prepare all students to benefit from the meaningful and challenging work within the CCSS, teachers need to create a growth mindset culture in the classroom. What kinds of cognitive exercises will she need, the types of readings? Dweck's (2010) research has shown that praising students for the process they have engaged in, the effort they applied, the strategies they used, the choices they made, and the persistence they displayed has yielded long-term benefits for student learning. A growth mindset philosophy is essential for educators to build a safe, productive classroom climate for learning and a sense of belonging for all students.

Finally, no solutions can be seriously considered without valuing and using the expertise that resides in the school and the teamwork needed to bring it to bear on Denise's issues. High schools are the final frontier for our students—tough times for all students, especially for Denise. Recognizing that no high school can be regarded as truly effective when it has students like Denise who cannot read, leaders must see the child, recognize the symptoms, and act quickly and decisively on multiple fronts. It can be done.

References

About the Standards. (n.d.). *Common Core State Standards Initiative.* Retrieved from http://www.corestandards.org/about-the-standards

Ayres, K. M., Maguire, A., & McClimon, D. (2009). Acquisition and generalization of chained tasks taught with computer-based video instruction to children with autism. *Education and Training in Mental Retardation and Developmental Disabilities, 44*, 493–508.

Bolt, S., & Roach, A. T. (2009). *Inclusive assessment and accountability: A guide to accommodations for students with diverse needs.* New York, NY: Guilford Press.

Browder, D., Ahlgrim-Delzell, L., Courtade-Little, G., & Snell, M. (2006). General curriculum access. In M. E. Snell & F. Brown (Eds.), *Instruction of students with severe disabilities* (6th ed., pp. 489–525). Upper Saddle River, NJ: Pearson.

Browder, D., Ahlgrim-Delzell, L., Spooner, F., & Baker, J. (2009). Using time delay to teach literacy to students with severe developmental disabilities. *Exceptional Children, 75*, 343–364.

Browder, D. M., Jimenez, B. A., & Trela, K. (2012). Grade-aligned math instruction for secondary students with moderate intellectual disability. *Education and Training in Autism and Developmental Disabilities, 47*, 373–388.

Browder, D. M., Spooner, F., Ahlgrim-Delzell, L., Wakeman, S. Y., & Harris, A. (2008). A meta-analysis for teaching mathematics to individuals with significant cognitive disabilities. *Exceptional Children, 74*, 404–432.

Brownell, M. T., Mellard, D. F., & Deshler, D. D. (1993). Differences in the learning and transfer performance between students with learning disabilities and other low-achieving students on problem-solving tasks. *Learning Disability Quarterly, 16*(2), 136–156.

Bulgren, J. A., Graner, P. S., & Deshler, D. D. (2013). Literacy challenges and opportunities for students with learning disabilities in social studies and history. *Learning Disabilities Research and Practices, 28*(1), 17–27.

Camara, W., & Quenemoen, R. (2012). *Defining and measuring college and career readiness and informing the level of performance level descriptors (PLDs)*. Washington, DC: Partnership for Assessment of Readiness for College and Careers. Retrieved from https://research.collegeboard.org/sites/default/files/publications/2012/7/presentation-2012-3-developing-performance-level-descriptors-criteria.pdf.

Carter, E. W., Ditchman, N., Sun, Y., Trainor, A. A., Swedeen, B., & Owens, L. (2010). Summer employment and community experience of transition-age youth with severe disabilities. *Exceptional Children, 76*, 194–212.

CAST. (2011). *Universal Design for Learning Guidelines 2.0*. Wakefield, MA: CAST.

Catch 'gap students' during transition to Common Core (2014), Special Education Report, 40(6). Palm Beach Gardens, FL: LRP Publications.

Cobb, P., & Jackson, K. (2011). Assessing the quality of the common core state standards for mathematics. *Educational Research, 40*, 183–185.

Cole, R. W. (2008). *Educating everybody's children: Diverse teaching strategies for diverse learners* (2nd ed.). Alexandria, VA: ASCD.

Cortiella, C., & Burnette, J. (2009). *Challenging change: How schools and districts are improving the performance of special education students*. New York, NY: National Center for Learning Disabilities.

Courtade, G., Browder, D. M., & Spooner, F. (2010). Training teachers to use an inquiry-based task analysis to teach science to students with moderate and severe disabilities. *Education and Training in Autism and Developmental Disabilities, 45*, 378–399.

Courtade, G., Spooner, F., Browder, D., & Jimenez, B. (2012). Seven reasons to promote a standards-based instruction for students with severe disabilities: A reply to Ayres, Lowrey, Douglas, & Sievers (2011). *Education and Training in Autism and Developmental Disabilities, 47*, 3–13.

Courtade-Little, G., & Browder, D. M. (2005). *Aligning IEPs with academic standards for students with moderate and severe disabilities*. Verona, WI: Attainment Company.

Darling-Hammond, L., & Adamson, F. (2010). *Beyond basic skills: The role of performance assessment in achieving 21st century standards of learning*. Stanford, CA: Stanford Center for Opportunity Policy in Education (SCOPE).

Deconstruct standards to align IEP goals with Common Core (2014). Special Education Report, 40(6). Palm Beach Gardens, FL: LRP Publications.

Deshler, R. T., Deshler, D. D., & Biancarosa, G. (2007). School and district change to improve adolescent literacy. In D. D. Deshler, A. S. Palincsar, G. Biancarosa, & M. Nair (Eds.), *Informed choices for struggling adolescent readers: A research-based guide to instructional programs and practices*. Newark, DE: International Reading Association.

DiCecco, V., & Gleason, M. (2002). Using graphic organizers to attain relational knowledge from expository text. *Journal of Learning Disabilities, 35*(4), 306–331.

Dolman, D. (2013). The Common Core standards: Why they matter to teachers and parents of children with hearing loss. *Listening and Spoken Language Knowledge Center*. Retrieved from http://www.listeningandspokenlanguage.org/CommonCoreStandards.aspx

Dweck, C. S. (2010). Even geniuses work hard. *Educational Leadership, 68*(1), 16–20.

Gamm, S., Elliott, J., Wright Halbert, J. W., Price-Baugh, R., Hall, R., Walston, D., . . . Casserly, M. (2012). *Common Core State Standards and diverse urban students: Using multi-tiered systems of support*. Washington, DC: Council of the Great City Schools.

Gulamhussein, A. (2013). *Teaching the teachers: Effective professional development in an era of high stakes accountability*. Alexandria, VA: Center for Public Education. Retrieved from http://www.centerforpubliceducation.org/Main-Menu/Staffingstudents/Teaching-the-Teachers-Effective-Professional-Development-in-an-Era-of-High-Stakes-Accountability/Teaching-the-Teachers-Full-Report.pdf

Haager, D., & Vaughn, S. (2013). The common core state standards and reading: Interpretations and implications for elementary students with learning disabilities. *Learning Disabilities Research and Practice, 28*(1), 5–16.

Heifetz, R. A., & Linsky, M. (2002). *Leadership on the line*. Boston, MA: Harvard Business School Press.

Individuals with Disabilities Education Act (IDEA), 20 U.S.C. § 1400 (2004a).

Individuals with Disabilities Education Act (IDEA), 108-446 (2004b). Retrieved from http://www.copyright.gov/legislation/pl108-446.pdf

Individuals with Disabilities Education Act (IDEA), 34 C.F.R. § 300.105 (2004c). Retrieved from http://www.ecfr.gov/cgi-bin/text-idx?SID=d4df849276feb0226a9f7a5b4a47422b&node=se34.2.300_1105&rgn=div8

Johnson, S. M., Berg, J. H., & Donaldson, M. L. (2005). *Who stays in teaching and why: A review of the literature on teacher retention*. Cambridge, MA: Harvard Graduate School of Education.

Jorgensen, C. (2005). The least dangerous assumption: The challenge to create a new paradigm. *Disability Solution, 6*(3), 1, 5–9, 15.

Kleinert, H., Kearns, J., Quenemoen, R., & Thurlow, M. (2013). *Alternate assessments based on common core state standards: How do they relate to college and career readiness?* (NCSC GSEG Policy Paper). Minneapolis, MN: University of Minnesota, National Center and State Collaborative.

Laitusis, C. C., & Cook, L. L. (2007). *Large scale assessment and accommodations: What works?* Arlington, VA: Council for Exceptional Children.

Maxwell, L. A. (2014, August). U.S. school enrollment hits majority-minority milestone. *Education Week, 34*(1). Retrieved from http://www.edweek.org/ew/articles/2014/08/20/01demographics.h34.html

McColl, A. (2005). Tough call: Is no child left behind constitutional? *Phi Delta Kappan, 86*(8), 64.

McLaughlin, M. J. (2012, September). Access for all: Six principles for principals to consider in accessing the common core for students with disabilities. *Principal*, 22–26.

Moats, L. (2012, Fall). Reconciling the common core state standards with reading research. *Perspectives on Language and Literacy*, 15–18.

National Council of Teachers of Mathematics. (2000). *Principles and standards for school mathematics*. Reston, VA: National Council of Teachers of Mathematics.

No Child Left Behind (NCLB) Act of 2001, Pub. L. No. 107-110, § 115, Stat. 1425 (2002).

Nolet, V., & McLaughlin, M. J. (2005). *Accessing the general curriculum: Including students with disabilities in standards-based reform* (2nd ed.). Thousand Oaks, CA: Corwin Press.

Olson, C. B., & Land, R. (2007). A cognitive strategies approach to reading and writing instruction for English language learners in secondary school. *Research in the Teaching of English, 41*(3). Retrieved from http://www.jstor.org/stable/40171732

Porter, A., McMaken, J., Hwang, J., & Yang, R. (2011). Common core standards: The new US intended curriculum. *Educational Research, 40*, 103–116.

Powell, S. R., Fuchs, L. S., & Fuchs, D. (2013). Reaching the mountaintop: Addressing the common core standards in mathematics for students with mathematical difficulties. *Learning Disabilities Research and Practice, 28*(1), 38–48.

Quenemoen, R. (2008). *A brief history of alternate assessments based on alternate achievement standards* (Synthesis Report 68). Minneapolis, MN: National Center on Educational Outcomes.

Samuels, C. A. (2011). Special educators look to align IEPs to Common-Core standards. *Education Week, 30*(15), 8–9.

Schaffhauser, D. (2013, January 1). Assistive tech goes mainstream. *Education Digest, 79*(4), 51–56.

Section 504 of the Rehabilitation Act, 34 C.F.R. § 104 (1973).

Sousa, D. A., & Tomlinson, C. A. (2011). *Differentiation and the brain: How neuroscience supports the learner-friendly classroom.* Bloomington, IN: Solution Tree Press.

Spooner, F., Browder, D., & Mims, P. (2011). Evidence-based practices. In D. Browder & F. Spooner (Eds.), *Teaching students with moderate and severe disabilities* (pp. 92–122). New York, NY: Guilford Press.

Stoll, L., Bolam, R., McMahon, A., Wallace, M., & Thomas, S. (2006). Professional learning communities: A review of the literature. *Journal of Educational Change, 7*(4), 221–258.

Swanson, H. L., & Deshler, D. (2003). Instructing adolescents with learning disabilities: Converting a meta-analysis to practice. *Journal of Learning Disabilities, 36*, 124–35.

Telfer, D. M. (2012). *A synthesis of lessons learned: How districts used assessment and accountability to increase performance for students with disabilities as part of district-wide improvement.* Minneapolis, MN: University of Minnesota, National Center on Educational Outcomes.

Thurlow, M. L. (2010, April). *ESEA reauthorization: Standards and assessments* (Oral Testimony). United States Senate, Health, Education, Labor and Pensions Committee (HELP), Washington, DC (As cited by: Thurlow, M. L. (2013). Common core for all—reaching the potential of students with disabilities. *Social Policy Report, 28*(2), 18–20).

Thurlow, M. L. (2012). Common Core State Standards: The promise and the peril for students with disabilities. *The Special Edge, 25*(3), 1, 6–8.

Thurlow, M. L. (2013). Common core for all—reaching the potential of students with disabilities. *Social Policy Report, 28*(2), 18–20.

Towles-Reeves, E., Kearns, J., Kleinert, H., & Kleinert, J. (2009). An analysis of the learning characteristics of students taking alternate assessments based on alternate achievement standards. *Journal of Special Education, 42*, 241–254.

Tschannen-Moran, M., & Hoy, A. W. (2001). Teacher efficacy: Capturing an elusive construct. *Teaching and Teacher Education, 17*(7), 783–805.

Universal Design for Learning. (n.d.). *CAST.* Retrieved from http://www.cast.org

U.S. Department of Education, National Center for Education Statistics. (2014). *The nation's report card: Mathematics* (NCES 2010-451). Washington, DC: National Center for Education Statistics, Institute of Education Sciences. Retrieved from: http://nces.ed.gov/programs/coe/indicator_cgg.asp

Wakeman, S., Karvonen, M., & Ahumada, A. (2013). Changing instruction to increase achievement for students with moderate to severe intellectual disabilities. *Teaching Exceptional Children, 46*(2), 6–13.

CHAPTER

The Common Core Standards, UDL, RTI

Marriage, Merger, Partnership

Christopher O'Brien, Gloria D. Campbell-Whatley, Ozalle Toms, and Christie L. Felder

Christine is in the seventh grade and has difficulty with impulsivity control and is frustrated easily. She demonstrates inappropriate social skills when she gets frustrated and may curse or scream at teachers or other students and may even throw things when angered. She functions one year below grade level in reading and math. She works well with younger students and exhibits strong leadership skills with them. She uses her phone, listens to her MP3 player, plays on Facebook or Twitter, and puts on make-up in class. The teachers overall use lecture, the textbook, and board work as their main teaching tools. Homework and classwork is assigned from the textbook. At this school, students have unit exams and pop quizzes each week. So how can we merge Universal Design for Learning, Response to Intervention, and the CCSS for this student?

Introduction

Hehir (2006) suggests that the natural consequence of inclusive education and more recent policy changes is an urgent dialogue regarding the need for schools to change in order to achieve the lofty goal of providing access to the general curriculum for students with disabilities. Schools must change in ways that allow a more proactive means of addressing diverse student needs. Although American public schools were not designed to address student diversity, schools must now adapt to a wider range of student needs, particularly in the areas of reading development and behavior management. Educational leaders are uniquely positioned to design schoolwide systems that respond to learner diversity.

Universal Design for Learning (UDL) is the term that is often used to reflect a broad paradigm shift regarding the manner in which schools plan to address the goals of inclusion. In the broadest terms, UDL represents a perspective that emphasizes the reduction of barriers to learning in school. Increasing access to standardized, rigorous curricula for a student population that has increasingly diverse needs requires strong leadership, planning, and strategic, systematic efforts to preemptively address "special needs" that exist in schools prior to those needs becoming "problems" or "barriers." Although the term UDL implies "universality," two general misconceptions or challenges that arise in professional dialogue about UDL. The term does not imply that district leaders or building administrators should adopt a "singular" curriculum to teach everyone the same way. In fact, the term implies tremendous flexibility in teaching and learning experiences anticipating learner differences, such that schools can be more efficient and *reduce the need for highly specialized and separate educational programs* that reflect the historical function of special education. Another challenge associated with this term is the need for translation of instructional principles that reflect universal design to actual programs, lesson plans, and technological developments that can truly address *every* learner need. Ultimately, it is not a simple outcome but guides practice as an idealistic end-goal—the goal that may never be reached but represents a good aim.

UDL is premised on the need for an instructional response to "inclusive education" and will require schools to function in a substantially different way than they have in the past. Included in this shift will be a focus on prevention of failure—a notion consistent with models of Multi-tiered Systems of Support (MTSS), Response to Intervention (RTI) for academics, and Schoolwide Positive Behavior Support. Prevention of academic and behavioral problems requires a system that is bigger and better resourced than special education. UDL reflects broad systemic changes that include differences in thinking from the level of the school district leadership, to building school leaders, to the level of the practicing teacher, particularly in the earliest grades. Collaboration among a team of professionals, including learning and behavior specialists and interventionists (special education teachers), associated support personnel (speech language pathologists, assistive technologists, therapists), and general education teachers, is the starting point for actualizing the potential of UDL. This kind of rich collaboration must be effectively coordinated by clear school policy and administrative leadership.

Although there is considerable jargon and a vast set of theoretical models that claim to represent the necessary changes in education, it is important in the case of UDL to see how other programs may reflect similar philosophies. Hehir (2006) includes discussions of RTI as a component of a larger UDL framework. To be clear, UDL can be seen, simultaneously, as a broad framework for school reform and accessibility and a model for teaching at the classroom level that reflects clear planning for learner differences. Rather than reacting or "retro-fitting" for learner difficulties, classroom-level UDL implementation tends to emphasize a proactive plan for instructional design in which learner supports and modifications have been embedded in the instructional process. Further, both instructional technologies and assistive technologies (i.e., technology designed to compensate for the weaknesses of children with disabilities) offer unique advantages in designing instruction and instructional materials that reflect UDL principles.

UDL is an instructional framework premised on the notion that schools must *proactively* design instruction in response to rigorous curricula with the assumption of student diversity. UDL involves an emphasis on integrating specialized instruction and accessible materials into general teaching practices. Federal legislation has been a driving force behind the expansion of UDL, typically with an emphasis on technology innovation to promote access and overcome previously fixed barriers to the curriculum (O'Brien, Aguinaga, & Mundorf, 2009). A lofty goal, UDL assumes that learning experiences will be designed such that instruction benefits students of all abilities, interests, and backgrounds (Blue, 2010; Rose & Meyer, 2002; Salazar, 2010). From a leadership perspective, this instructional design concept is an overarching framework for teaching that aligns well with the current diversity of students in public schools (i.e., very diverse backgrounds, learning needs, learning preferences, and academic abilities/disabilities). School and special education leaders will act as forerunners to promote universal design while finding ways to circumvent the barriers in the process. Leaders will need to be instrumental in providing resources to design instructional experiences in schools that will be accessible to all students. This is difficult to do, but technology, in particular, makes it more likely.

Rose and Meyer (2002) refer to three core principles of UDL: multiple means of representation, multiple means of expression, and multiple means of engagement (Table 8.1).

Although the principles of UDL mentioned here are important, according to Edyburn (2005), UDL first and foremost seeks to reduce barriers for everyone.

Table 8.1 Three Core Principles of UDL

Multiple means of representation	Provide multiple and flexible processes for acquiring new knowledge in the classroom. Consider how a concept could be best taught. Is the textbook or printed material the best and only way to teach a concept in your class? Could a video clip or other multimedia tool represent the concept more effectively to a broader audience that may not thrive in a text-driven classroom?
Multiple means of expression	Provide a variety of options for students to demonstrate competence regarding a learning objective. Again, consider technological solutions and means of representing knowledge that are not limited to writing assignments.
Multiple means of engagement	Consider issues of interest, preference, and motivation when designing instruction. The opportunity to make choices or emphasize an area of interest can positively impact student performance.

Accessibility to rigorous and engaging learning experiences with the Common Core standards is a fundamental goal. UDL sets the tone that the curriculum should be modified or differentiated until it reaches as many students as possible, rather than declaring that children who do not thrive in the curriculum are disabled. Rather, books and instruction could be considered disabled if they are not able to meet the learning needs of most or all students. Further, from an efficiency standpoint, accessible instructional design is preferable over the need to create retrofits or awkward accommodations. For example, if six students in a class have substantial difficulty with notetaking, we might make special accommodations for each of those students. From a UDL standpoint, it might make more sense to anticipate problems with notetaking and teach all of the students a shortened strategy for effective notetaking in your class. You might also provide "guided notes" in which students simply fill in the blanks for key concepts. These tactics benefit the students who experience difficulty listening and taking notes, provide an accommodation, and focus attention on those concepts that are most relevant.

UDL stems from certain assumptions about student diversity—essentially, that it is natural for students in our classrooms to differ from each other in a number of ways. Ultimately, UDL is the instructional response to inclusive classrooms. Classrooms today include students with disabilities, varying background experiences, levels of motivation, as well as cultural/linguistic differences. Furthermore, most students served by special education have primarily "academic disabilities," and if we are to be consistent with the thinking of RTI, it simply makes sense to anticipate diversity of ability in academic contexts so that we can prepare for it. We can preempt difficulty rather than retrofitting. Often, students whose abilities or learning profiles are inconsistent with the design of instruction in school will fall behind and become marginalized by the overall educational system. A UDL vision would suggest that the curriculum must be flexible—allowing all students, including those in the margins, to access needed support.

Infusing UDL and the Common Core

So how does UDL relate to the Common Core? Essentially, the CCSS account for "what" we are responsible for teaching in American public schools whose states have adopted the standards. UDL, however, is a theoretical and/or philosophical orientation toward the "means of teaching" or the "how" of teaching regardless of the standards being examined (National Center for Universal Design for Learning, 2015). Consistently challenging in the examination of UDL is the notion that it applies to children with disabilities, as it has origins in special education research and is referenced in disability policy including the Individuals with Disabilities Education Act (IDEA 2004) and the Higher Education Opportunity Act (2008); however, as the CCSS are for everyone, UDL applies to everyone. In other words, UDL applies to the need to teach the rigorous CCSS to inclusive core classrooms comprised of heterogeneous groups. The essential elements of alignment between the thinking of UDL and the expectations of the CCSS revolve around the need for goals/standards to clarify the understanding that we want students to develop without predetermining or prejudging how students will acquire that knowledge. There must always be opportunity for students to receive multiple representations without multiple ways of demonstrating mastery of content. The tendency to mix the goals with the means to achieve those goals can be complicated based on the level of school and the ways in which standards are written (National Center for Universal Design for Learning, 2015). For example, standards related to written expression could be problematic for UDL philosophy, if the standards explicitly restrict learning outcomes to include the physical act of writing. If a student could not physically write, but could use dictation software, they may in fact develop their skills in expressive language despite the fact that they are not traditionally writing the words with a pencil on paper.

Effective Teaching Practices and Access to the General Curriculum

Several authors summarize *best academic practices* for inclusion and reaching students with mild or high-incidence disabilities noting that such practices are not necessarily limited to achievement in content areas but must extend to management of behavior and enhancement of social skills, which underlie the potential for academic success (King-Sears, 1997). Best practices include, but are not limited to, the following: (1) peer-mediated instruction, (2) strategy instruction, using the explicit, intensive model of instruction, (3) differentiated instruction, (4) self-determination, (5) explicit or direct instruction, particularly for more structured content, (6) curriculum-based assessment, (7) generalization techniques, (8) collaboration between general and special education, and (9) proactive behavior management (Sugai & Horner, 2006). Authors emphasize the need to integrate these approaches in teacher planning for diversity. From a non-technological perspective, one could recognize the need to use multiple strategies in a coordinated fashion to address unique learning needs and academic profiles over time. The coordinated implementation of general curriculum enhancements to instructional delivery and learning and behavioral supports is in fact a vision for universal design.

Leaders will need to suggest, manage, and institute and establish many practices in special education for service delivery (see Table 8.2) and reflect the non-technological potential for high -quality instruction to provide multiple means of recognition, expression, and engagement. Notable in each of these approaches are processes that overlap in activity of the different learning networks. In essence, a strategy that provides multiple access points and multiple means of recognition may also provide students with support in expression and thereby lead to higher levels of engagement. UDL, however, is not just traditional teaching. The methods discussed in Table 8.2 suggest an anticipated repertoire of instructional strategies and service delivery options necessary to proactively design curricula with the assumption of a broad a range of learning abilities, preferences, and needs.

Table 8.2 Effective Teaching Strategies

Differentiated instruction	Edyburn (2008) suggests that the models of *differentiated instruction* (discussed further in Chapter 9) and UDL are highly consistent with the emphasis being the proactive design of materials and learning environments anticipating learner differences. Unique to *differentiated instruction* is a strong emphasis on tiered lessons and the differentiation of content, process, and product (Hall, Strangman, & Meyer, 2003; Tomlinson, 2001).
Collaborative instruction and co-teaching	This instructional practice is typically referred to as cooperative teaching or co-teaching and involves the collaborative partnership between a general educator acting as a content specialist and a special educator acting as a specialist in instruction for students with disabilities (Bauwens & Hourcade, 1991; Cook & Friend, 1995).
Strategic instruction	The strategic instruction model (www.ku-crl.org) is an approach which assists students in overcoming areas of deficit in their skill repertoire and improving their metacognitive practices to improve performance in academic content. The larger collection of these learning strategies is referred to as the Learning Strategies Curriculum and includes a continuum of strategies to address skills in acquisition of knowledge, storage, or maintenance of knowledge and expression or demonstration of knowledge. Strategies in this curriculum include strategies for reading comprehension (e.g., word identification, paraphrasing), memorization of information (e.g., FIRST-letter mnemonic, LINCS vocabulary), expression of information (e.g., sentence writing, paragraph writing), and demonstration of competence (e.g., test-taking) which have been shown to be effective in improving student learning and performance (Lenz, Deshler, & Kissam, 2004).
Content enhancements	These routines are meant to enhance whole-group instruction, typically the instruction provided by general education teachers in inclusive classrooms. Two common examples of content enhancements are use of graphic organizers and mnemonic instruction, both strongly established in the special education literature.
Active student response (ASR)	The term ASR refers to observable, measurable, curriculum-related response to teacher-posed questions or instructions. An extensive research base demonstrates the relationship between increased ASR and student achievement. Three easy-to-implement strategies that promote ASR include (1) guided notes, (2) response cards, and (3) peer tutoring (Heward, 2006).
Peer support	A general term for a collection of inclusive practices to support students with disabilities in the general education classroom (Maheady, Harper, & Mallette, 2001) such as peer-mediated instruction (Fuchs, Fuchs, Mathes, & Simmons, 1997; Greenwood & Delquadri, 1995; Maheady, 1988; Maheady et al., 2001), classwide peer tutoring, peer-assisted learning strategies, and reciprocal teaching which refers to a collection of instructional strategies which require class members to work in reciprocal tutoring pairs as they compete with other teams (Greenwood & Delquadri, 1995).

No Tears for the Tiers: RTI and MTSS

MTSS is defined as a data-driven intervention and proactive-based structure for academic and behavioral systems through a layered continuum of research-based practices and systems (Benner, Kutash, Nelson, & Fisher, 2013). RTI, a multi-tiered system, is defined as a manner in which students at risk for academic failure and behavior challenges are identified and evidence-based interventions are provided at three levels of intensity (defined in Table 8.3) (Fuchs & Fuchs, 2007). Various measures determine if the student had a positive response to the intervention

Table 8.3 RTI Tiers

Tier 1	Students are universally screened for academic and behavioral challenges. Those with challenges receive evidence-based differentiated instruction for about six to eight weeks in the general education classroom. Results of the intervention are monitored and measured. If the student responds positively, they remain in Tier 1; if not, they are moved to Tier 2.
Tier 2	Interventions are modified, tailored, adapted, and personalized to the unique needs of targeted learners who did not respond positively to the instruction in Tier 1. The intervention is more intense and the instruction is administered a longer time (approximately 5 to 6 months) and aligned to the specific needs of the student. Just as in Tier 1, the students' progress is measured and monitored; if the student improves, they may stay in Tier 2 or be moved to Tier 1 and continue in the general education setting; if not, they are moved to Tier 3.
Tier 3	When a student doesn't respond to Tier 2 interventions, this level provides more intensive and individualized intervention. At this level, students are referred and identified for special education and 504 services. Students are provided individual diagnostic-type assessments to formulate an individualized instructional plan. Under IDEA, students may be evaluated by a multidisciplinary team to determine if a disability exists if improvements in behavior and academic task do not occur.

("Response to Interventions," 2013). This process was included as an option in the Individual's with Disabilities Education Act (2004) to identify children with specific learning disabilities rather than a discrepancy score between intellectual and academic ability. Supposedly, it is a general education initiative, but in actuality it is fuelled by special education leaders.

School Environmental Challenges and Solutions: Smoothing Rough Places

The main purpose of the CCSS is to identify the knowledge and skills student must acquire to be successful in a chosen college or career (Kendall, 2011). Despite complaints that CCSS robs teachers of having autonomy in the classroom, the CCSS only guides "what" students should be learning. McLaughlin (2012) recommends the implementation of the CCSS begin with the characteristics of students in mind. Students have different needs which require different accommodations and modifications to help them access the curriculum. Leaders need to ensure that teachers are able to understand and apply the principles by:

- beginning schoolwide assessments that measure needs, progress, and growth using both these approaches;

- setting expectations so that teachers clearly understand and use the RTI and UDL practices; and

- support the alignment of Individualized Education Programs (IEPs) with RTI, UDL, and CCSS.

Defining the Trinity: UDL, RTI, and CCSS

School and special education leaders must ensure that general and special education teachers are providing relevant instruction, using research-based interventions, appropriate materials, and teaching methods to help students move toward college or career readiness. RTI is a process for making educational decisions based on student's success or failure during specialized intervention, while UDL incorporates a variety of options for presentation of content and diversity of materials. Both provide a positive system based on research-based practices to promote meaningful educational results for students at all grade levels. Basham, Israel, Graden, Poth, and Winston (2010) define the merger of RTI and UDL as an ecological system, that is, the two concepts form a network of interactions in the social environment to provide practical interventions for students. School and special education leaders can facilitate using RTI and UDL in unison because both approaches have the following:

- Have shared objectives and educational outcomes; when used collectively, they can produce good results.

- Are based on a proactive model rather than a deficit model, providing appropriate instruction for all students, no matter the academic or behavioral level.

- Emphasize that intervention strategies are not "one size fits all" and are tailored to fit the specific needs of the student.

- Emphasize the need for frequent progress monitoring providing information to improve instruction.

- Utilize formative and curriculum-based assessments to ascertain the effectiveness of instructional methods and interventions.

- Can be used for both behaviorally and academically challenged students (Benner et al., 2013; Johnson-Harris & Mundschenk, 2014).

- Reduce barrier to instruction through technology, multiple means of representation, and proactive research-based interventions engaging students through several means.

School-Based Leaders

Teachers will need to know how to apply interventions in a consistent manner. Leaders will need to stress the symbiotic relationship between the UDL and RTI and present professional development in that manner. Having a proactive-based school in mind, school leaders will need to determine what kinds of supports are needed, the various research and data needed to make decisions, and the level or degree of integration of UDL and multi-tiered supports. Most of all, leaders will need to determine the types of measures that will be needed to define the success of implementation. School leaders will need to appraise the following:

- In order to expand instructional and behavioral practices, functional teams within the school should consider up-to-date research along with recent data to expand instructional and behavior practices. Collaborative grade-level teaming common for CCSS practices should be used to modify and strengthen practices for individual learners.

- Core instructional practices for beginning tiers should include flexible grouping and ongoing formative assessment measure. Instruction should be built into the core practices in the classroom. Differentiated methods such as direct explicit instruction (see Chapter 9) can be used in conjunction with scaffolding techniques. Tutoring and coaching sessions for students are recommended.

- Familiarize teachers on the use of assistive technology and encourage its use (Lowrey and Basham, 2010).

- Introduce the notion that MTSS can be used not only with students at risk or students with disabilities but also with English language learners (see Chapter 5).

Special Education Leaders

The increased rigor of expectations included in the CCSS has raised questions about how to best assist students with disabilities and provide access to the general curriculum (Haager and Vaughn, 2013). Although MTSS are seen as a general education initiative, special education leaders will need to spearhead the use and application of these methods. Special education leaders will need to be more involved with the assistive technology side of UDL as it is a must for many students with severe disabilities (discussed further in Chapter 8) and for those students placed in Tier 3 interventions. Special education leaders will need to:

- Encourage the effective use of data from several assessment measures so that teachers will make informed decisions about gaps in instruction for learners who are struggling.

- Use more aggressive measures of assistive individualized technology supports for students with severe disabilities, especially if their standards-based IEPs result in an infusion of various disciplines within the CCSS.

- Encourage teachers to use multiple ways to show mastery of content.

- Provide assistive technology specialist, related service personnel, etc., in order to support general and special educators.

- Develop a clear understanding of the grade-level expectations in the general education curriculum and identify necessary modifications.

- Devise a plan to collaborate with general education teachers and related service providers in order to design appropriate instruction.

- Infuse opportunities for guided practices in integrated lessons.

Applying the Common Core Standards and Solutions

What does behavior have to do with CCSS? Behavior and academics are intricately connected. Conroy, Sutherland, Haydon, Stormont, and Harmon (2008) found that students with disruptive behavior had significantly lower rates of acting out behavior when engaged in instruction! Instruction cannot occur unless the student is paying attention (Benner et al., 2013). Students with inappropriate behavior have unsuitable work habits, have less than desirable relationships with teachers, and can be inattentive during lessons. Many of these students, in any Tier, may require direct instruction to keep them engaged. For example, a student who has a short attention span or is easily distracted has been assigned the task to read an informational text and write a report. UDL can provide several choices for assignment completion: (a) listening to the text, (b) using text-to-speech technology, (c) writing the report using a computer, (d) giving the report orally, (e) designing a project, (f) recording it, (g) acting out the concept, (h) writing a script, or other methods to adapt instruction from traditional lessons.

When considering RTI and UDL for behavior purposes, school leaders will need to ask themselves (Lamar-Dukes, 2009):

- What are the multiple, varied means that students in this school can demonstrate their learning?
- What learning experiences do I want students to have?
- How can the school use technology in assignments and assessments?

Connections to Assessment

McAssey (2014) recommends the use of data-driven instruction to promote the implementation of the CCSS. Leaders will need to collect and analyze data from multiple sources of multi-tiered approaches to determine what methods and strategies might better support CCSS.

Keller-Margulis (2012) stated that fidelity or treatment integrity on intervention implementation is important when trying to determine what treatments were effective or most ineffective. Procedural integrity is the consistency of the plans, procedures, and steps of a student moving through the multi-tiered system. These steps are closely monitored. Leaders can use a protocol approach for Tier 1 to assure that the whole school is assessed. This option uses one validated intervention selected by the school team to improve the academic skills of its struggling students. Because a single, consistent intervention is used, it is easier to ensure accurate implementation or treatment fidelity. Tiers 2 and 3, however, may use a problem-solving approach that is more suited for students at risk or students with disabilities. At each tier teacher teams: (a) identify the problem and determine its cause, (b) develop a plan to address the problem, (c) implement the plan, and (d) evaluate the plan's effectiveness.

Data should be collected using a multi-method approach, including both direct and indirect measures. Data should be collected in a consistent manner with the same frequency, duration, and intensity needed according to the protocol, and students move through the system as intended. Indirect methods include a review of self-reports, checklist, etc. from staff. Direct methods include observation of the assessments, intervention, and decision-making activities. Both methods are feasible and can produce more accurate results (Keller-Margulis, 2012).

Research-Based Practical Tips and Caveats

In order to implement an effective MTSS or any multi-tiered system, leaders need to do the following:

- Form school-based grade-level teams that devise and/or determine

  - formative assessments,
  - evidence- and research-based interventions, and
  - methods of progress monitoring.

- Define methods for the teams to gather and analyze behavioral and academic school data and place students in tiers and determine a consistent manner in which they transition to and from tiers.

- Set priorities, goals, and a timeline.

- Infuse UDL into the tiered interventions identified for each tier level and grade level.

- Follow the suggestions determined by Staskowski, Hardin, Klein, and Wozniak (2012) for lesson planning using UDL for the CCSS to advise teacher instruction:

  - Use overarching ideas as they connect better with other disciplines.
  - Using inquiry questioning techniques, learning strategies, and opening statements to a lesson (mentioned in Chapter 9) helps students seek real-world and a more profound meaning to the lesson.
  - The use of formative assessments as mentioned in Chapter 9 provides feedback to the teacher and the learner, checks for understanding, and mastery of a concept.

- Decide on the fidelity of treatment and progress-monitoring methodologies.

- Make needed changes in the instruction and measures.

Summary

According to Kendall (2011), CCSS have a set of shared national standards that ensure the same level of expectations for every student in the country. MTSS and UDL offer students choices and access to a rigorous academic curriculum. Both offer a means of planning a curriculum with less barriers, more flexibility, and proactive strategies. MTSS exists to determine the power of a particular intervention at a particular level with academic and behavioral interventions. Let's see how Christine, who we visited at the beginning of the chapter, is faring in light of this increased flexibility provided by MTSS and UDL.

When last we visited Christine, she was busily putting on make-up in class in preparation for the class change that was ten minutes away. However, her teacher had stopped teaching two-thirds of the way through the period and instructed the students to begin their homework. Rather than redirect Christine, her teacher ignored her off-task behavior. Christine was diagnosed with behavioral issues and is receiving IDEA services. Although her IEP spells out that Christine be provided opportunities to work in groups with younger students at her grade level, and even though this is a multi-grade class, her teacher is leery of putting Christine with other kids given her past behavioral episodes. Therefore, Christine is not getting to demonstrate and build on her positive behaviors, so even though the class is ideal for learning groups, when Christine gets frustrated with lectures—much of which she does not understand—she acts out. The teacher calls the office. An assistant principal responds and Christine is removed ... again.

All schools and systems differ; therefore, leaders will need to form their own evidence and research-based approaches that fit the Christines in their schools and increase efforts to continue to explore more possible combinations of interventions and technologies.

References

Basham, J. D., Israel, M., Graden, J., Poth, R., & Winston, M. (2010, December 7). A comprehensive approach to RTI: Embedding universal design for learning and technology. *Learning Disability Quarterly, 33*(4), 243–255.

Bauwens, J., & Hourcade, J. J. (1991). Making co-teaching a mainstreaming strategy. *Preventing School Failure, 35,* 19–24.

Benner, G. J., Kutash, K., Nelson, J. R., & Fisher, M. B. (2013, August 1). Closing the achievement gap of youth with emotional and behavioral disorders through multi-tiered systems of support. *Education & Treatment of Children, 36,* 3.

Blue, E. (2010). UDL: Paving the way toward 21st century literacies for special needs learners. *School Talk, 15*(3), 1–3.

Conroy, M., Sutherland, K., Haydon, T., Stormont, M., & Harmon, J. (2009). Preventing and ameliorating young children's chronic problem behaviors: An ecological classroom-based approach. *Psychology in the Schools, 46,* 3–17.

Cook, L., & Friend, M. (1995). Co-teaching: Guidelines for creating effective practices. *Focus on Exceptional Children, 28,* 1–16.

Edyburn, D. (2005). Universal design for learning. *Special Education Technology Practice, 7*(5), 16–22.

Edyburn, D. L. (2008). *A primer on universal design (UD) in education.* Retrieved from https://pantherfile.uwm.edu/edyburn/www/ud.html#foundations

Fuchs, D., Fuchs, L. S., Mathes, P. G., & Simmons, D. C. (1997). Peer-assisted learning strategies: Making classrooms more responsive to diversity. *American Educational Research Journal, 34*(1), 174.

Fuchs, L. S., & Fuchs, D. (2007). A model for implementing response to intervention. *Teaching Exceptional Children,* 14–20.

Greenwood, C. R., Delquadri, J., & Hall, R. V. (1984). Opportunity to respond and student academic achievement. In W. L. Heward, T. E. Heron, D. S. Hill, & J. Trap-Porter (Eds.), *Focus on behavior analysis in education* (pp. 58–88). Upper Saddle River, NJ: Merrill/Prentice Hall.

Haager, D., & Vaughn, S. (2013). The common core state standards and reading: Interpretations and implications for elementary students with learning disabilities. *Learning Disability Research, 28,* 5–16.

Hall, T., Strangman, N., & Meyer, A. (2003). *Differentiated instruction and implications for UDL implementation.* Wakefield, MA: National Center on Accessing the General Curriculum. Retrieved from http://ok.gov/sde/sites/ok.gov.sde/files/DI_UDL.pdf

Hehir, T. (2006). *New direction in special education: Eliminating ableism in policy and practice.* Cambridge, MA: Harvard Education Press.

Heward, W. (2006). *Exceptional children: An introduction to special education* (8th ed.). Upper Saddle River, NJ: Prentice Hall.

Individuals with Disabilities Education Act of 2004, Pub. L. No. 108-446, 20 U.S.C. §§ 1400 et seq. (2004). Retrieved from https://www.govtrack.us/congress/bills/108/hr1350

Johnson-Harris, K. M., & Mundschenk, N. A. (2014, January 1). Working effectively with students with BD in a general education classroom: The case for universal design for learning. *Clearing House: A Journal of Educational Strategies, Issues and Ideas, 87*(4), 168–174.

Keller-Margulis, M. A. (2012). Fidelity of implementation framework: A critical need for response to intervention models. *Psychology in the Schools, 49*(4), 342–352.

Kendall, J. (2011). *Understanding Common Core State Standards.* Alexandria, VA: ASCD.

King-Sears, M. E. (1997). Best academic practices for inclusive classrooms. *Focus on Exceptional Children, 29,* 1–22.

Lamar-Dukes, P. (2009, September 1). Reaching the hard to reach: A review of an initiative aimed at increasing participation and supports for people of color with disabilities and their families in disability organizations. *Research & Practice for Persons with Severe Disabilities, 34*(3–4), 76–80.

Lenz, B. K., Deshler, D. D., & Kissam, B. R. (2004). *Teaching content to all: Evidence-based inclusive practices in middle and secondary schools.* Boston, MA: Pearson Education.

Lowrey, A. L., & Basham, J. D. (2010). Individualized education programs (IEPs). In T. C. Hunter, J. C. Carper, T. J. Lasley, & C. D. Raisch (Eds.), *Encyclopedia of educational reform and dissent.* Thousand Oaks, CA: Sage.

Maheady, L. (1988). Peer-mediated instruction: A promising approach to meeting the diverse needs of LD adolescents. *Learning Disability Quarterly, 11,* 108–113.

Maheady, L., Harper, G. F., & Mallette, B. (2001). Peer-mediated instruction and interventions and students with mild disabilities. *Remedial and Special Education, 22,* 4–14.

McAssey, L. (2014). Common Core assessments: A principal's view. *Principal,* 15–18. Retrieved from www.naesp.org

McLaughlin, M. J. (2012). Access for all: Six principles for principals to consider in implementing CCSS for students with disabilties. *Principal,* 22–26.

National Center for Universal Design for Learning (2015). Retrieved from http://www.udlcenter.org/

O'Brien, C., Aguinaga, N., & Mundorf, J. (2009, March). *Preparing the next generation of teachers to integrate special education technology in inclusive classrooms.* Proceedings of the 20th International Conference of the Society for Information Technology and Teacher Education (pp. 3189–3194). Charleston, SC.

Response to Interventions. (2013). *Center for parent information and resources.* Retrieved from http://www.parentcenterhub.org/repository/rti/

Rose, D. H., & Meyer, A. (2002). *Teaching every student in the digital age: Universal design for learning.* Alexandria, VA: Association for Supervision and Curriculum Development (ASCD).

Salazar, P. (2010). In this issue. *NASSP Bulletin, 94*(1), 3–4.

Staskowski, M., Hardin, S., Klein, M., & Wozniak, C. (2012). Universal design for learning: Speech-language pathologists and their teams making the common core curriculum accessible. *Seminars in Speech and Language, 33*(2), 111–129. Retrieved from http://www.mm3admin.co.za/cms/cpd/articles/cd18d27e-bec5-4926-abbc-abdade8f1107.pdf

Sugai, G., & Horner, R. R. (2006, January 1). A promising approach for expanding and sustaining school-wide positive behavior support. *School Psychology Review, 35*(2), 245–259.

The Higher Education Opportunity Act of 2008, Pub. L. No. 110-315 (2008). Retrieved from https://www.govtrack.us/congress/bills/110/hr4137

Tomlinson, C. (2001). *How to differentiate instruction in mixed-ability classrooms* (2nd ed.). Alexandria, VA: ASCD Publications.

CHAPTER

Differentiating the Common Core Curriculum

Rebecca A. Shore, David M. Dunaway, and Gloria D. Campbell-Whatley

Chuang has been in the country for ten years. His parents passed away two years ago, and he has changed schools four times since then. Currently, he and his older brother live in a suburban setting with his present foster family, and Chuang is in the ninth grade at the local high school. Despite his present neighborhood setting, Chuang says he is interested in joining a gang and has become involved with a group of students from a nearby neighborhood with juvenile detention records. Although he attends school, he is disinterested in schoolwork and does not complete his assignments. He is very conversational, but has difficulty reading. His older brother is in the twelfth grade and is doing very well in the same school. He seems to "look up" to his brother, and his brother seems to care for him and acts as a surrogate parent at times.

Introduction

Differentiated instruction involves teaching students according to their specific needs and strengths while creating learning opportunities using varied methods rather than a more standardized approach. Chuang in the vignette is having difficulty reading and will need his instruction differentiated so that he may be college- and career-ready. Because each learner comes to school with a different profile of learning challenges and strengths on any given day (Chuang's brother has a very different profile), by varying instruction each individual student is placed at the center of learning, replacing teacher-centered instruction with student-centered instruction. This chapter explains differentiated instruction in relation to the Common Core curriculum from an administrative aspect and suggests ways for leaders to help teachers use differentiated techniques. Differentiated instruction is more than just being intuitive to improvise when confronted with student learning differences or day-to-day learning challenges; it is purposefully and strategically planning for those differences. For leaders, varied instructional methods linked to Common Core assessments are also discussed as related to core instruction.

Historical Relevance

The last century of delivering the service of educational instruction in the United States has evolved from increased access for more diverse students and federal funding to address equity issues to testing every child to assess learning and educator accountability. Many aspects of the provision of a free and appropriate public education system in the United States, however, have remained alarmingly similar. For example, grade-level distribution of students has been generally based on birthdates and a nationwide structure that typically begins with kindergarten and the expectation of the progression of student achievement each year from K through twelfth grade. Unfortunately, large numbers of American children have not successfully progressed through the system to earn a high school diploma.

Reform efforts include attempts to add a year of early childhood education, namely prekindergarten, to the traditional K–12 system. Research from the cognitive sciences and neurosciences suggests that the early years of life present the best opportunity to bridge learning gaps (Diamond & Hopson, 1999). At the same time, longitudinal studies of high school reform efforts have not revealed any silver bullet for increasing student learning or much success for the present delivery of instruction to all students systemwide (Shore, 1997). Consequently, the results from investigating the lack of learning gains for adolescents support this move to include the earliest childhood environments in our nation's education reform efforts when a greater impact may be made through interventions (Shore, 2002). The brain becomes less and less "plastic" as children reach puberty and by the high school years levels off in terms of brain activity (Diamond & Hopson, 1999). It stands to reason that some systemic reform efforts that focus on younger children make sense. Likewise, since "brain changes" through education becomes significantly more difficult in the teen years, the notion that one size could fit all of the variation needed to reach high schoolers seems implausible.

It is this same research area that revealed the importance of the early childhood educational environment and the difficulty of teaching the teen brain that has led to the revision of Benjamin Bloom's landmark publication of *A Taxonomy for Learning* in 2001 (Anderson et al., 2000). The original *Bloom's Taxonomy* levels from low to high—knowledge, comprehension, application, analysis, synthesis, and evaluation—were changed to *verbs*, better depicting actual brain functions which more accurately describe these levels of activity when the brain is engaged in thinking—remembering, understanding, applying, analyzing, evaluating, and creating. This deeper understanding of how we learn has fueled important recent reform efforts, the development and implementation of the CCSS for schools.

Reducing high school dropout rates and preparing *all* students for college work or with employable skills upon high school graduation is and has been a serious concern and is a focus for improving our present education system. As far back as the initial passage of the Elementary and Secondary Education Act of 1965, this focus has been a national education goal. Federal funds were doubled that decade to eliminate the effects of poverty and level the playing field for all children, and the percentage of education funding assistance has increased annually ever since. While some improvement in the dropout statistics has emerged in isolated instances over the years, still, an unacceptable number of students do not make it through our system to realize high school graduation. Perhaps influenced by the lackluster progress in improving secondary school learning achievement and increased interest in early childhood education to reduce the width of the achievement gap, this new external influence on the system comes as a means for providing clarity of purpose as well as for standardizing the outcomes of the system. The CCSS aim to define, at least to some degree, what we as a nation want our children to learn and be able to do upon leaving each of our states' different education systems.

The widespread adoption of this set of common standards offered to states across the country to more unify the purposes and outcomes of our 55-million-student-strong system is strong evidence that we still place a high value on educating all of our nation's children. The framework for the CCSS reflects a realization and acceptance that a one-size-fits-all approach does not fit all students learning K through 12; nor does only one teaching method ensure attainment of a specific end goal regardless of the content or goal clarity. We now recognize that student learning does not fit neatly into preset schedules, nor can it always be measured by bubbles on scantrons or excel spreadsheets; each child learns differently and at a different pace.

Rather than prescribing a specific means to an educational ends, the CCSS present just what the title suggests, set standards. And while the CCSS set rigorous content expectations for all students and connect those expectations to particular grade levels, they do not prescribe the means by which mastery of the standards are to be achieved. This flexibility has two levels. First, it allows districts, and in some cases school-based leaders, to make their own decisions for planning and equipping teachers to establish appropriate benchmarks for mastering the Common Core curriculum. For example, the CCSS emphasize but do not dictate curriculum or teaching methods. Just because topic A appears before topic B in the standards does not mean that topic A must be taught before topic B. On another level, the CCSS do not dictate a particular means by which to achieve the ends, mastery of the standards. Teachers are allowed to tailor instruction such that each child's needs for reaching the standards are met.

State- and/or district-level restrictions, however, can impede the most flexible of approaches. Some contracts or bargaining agreements can present obstacles to efforts such as doubling class time in math or school bell schedules. This is why leadership becomes a critical component to implementing the CCSS or any innovative reform effort or out-of-the-box approach to improving schools and is the focus of this chapter. Ironically, while the rigorous standards themselves are clearly articulated and are intended to provide standardization across the country through setting grade-level timelines, the methods by which they are actually met are widely varied and flexible.

As delineated in prior chapters, students are given the opportunity to master the core concepts within the standards beginning in the elementary grades and then progress strategically through grade 12. Since these CCSS have been introduced and applied across states in recent years, real and specific challenges have surfaced. School-based leaders have identified general problems with particular student populations not meeting the standards simultaneously or not meeting them at all. For example, some students in special education programs and students for whom English is not their primary language do not always progress at the same pace as their peers and have different needs than many of their peers. Consequently, teachers struggle with how, exactly, to ensure the success of each child. At the same time, the student population in the United States is becoming increasingly diverse and educators are being called upon to meet the needs of all children in order to ensure success for each student in their classrooms. For example, Chuang in the vignette is from a culturally and linguistically diverse background and seemingly has some difficulty in reading. His instruction will need to be addressed academically and culturally.

Setting high expectations for students is not new; however, the high expectations combined with high-stakes testing for all students is a more recent reform initiative. With teacher and administrator compensation attached to test scores in some cases today, there is an increased concern and focus by teachers and leaders to ensure that all students meet these rigorous standards. While students with disabilities are specifically noted within the standards, so also is the expectation for them to function to become college- or career-ready. Yet teachers and leaders wrestle with the expectation that all students will become proficient and tackle specifically how students with various learning styles and special needs will fair in the Common Core-based curriculum. It is important that evidence-based techniques that have a positive effect on students with disabilities or other learning differences be used as potential solutions to mastering the CCSS.

A plethora of old and new evidence-based instructional strategies are at work in America's classrooms today. Some are traditional, long-standing methods such as *explicit instruction* and *inquiry-based learning*. Other more recent practices in use such as inclusion, Response to Intervention (RTI)/Multi-tiered Systems of Support

(MTSS), and Universal Design for Learning (UDL) have been discussed in prior chapters. Regardless of any particular teacher's favorite instructional strategy in use in their classrooms, school-based leaders must work with all teachers to effectively and appropriately integrate and assess the CCSS into these processes.

One fact is well established through centuries of schooling. All children do not learn in the same ways or at the same rates. Students today enter our classrooms with a plethora of differences not only in ability, language, race, gender, learning preferences, and socioeconomic related factors, like Chuang, but also in their confidence levels regarding different curricular components or relationships with peers or adults. The variety is nearly infinite, and since it is human beings who we are teaching and not widgets that we are producing, each of these differences can influence learning in different ways. A one-size-fits-all model or strategy for any curricula is not likely to work well for all students. One approach, however, applied to any instructional strategy can increase the chances for success with reaching the CCSS (or any standards).

What Is Differentiated Instruction?

Differentiation is not a new concept in education. The one-room schoolhouse of the turn of the century where one teacher taught all students of school age, regardless of ability, all grouped in the same room, was actually an example of a differentiated classroom. According to Tomlinson (1999, 2001), differentiation refers to tailoring instruction to meet the individual needs of all students. Differentiating instruction creates a learning environment where students with diverse and different learning needs and abilities, and different ways of expressing what they have learned, can be successful and reach the same curricular goals. A differentiated classroom includes typical students of average and above-average ability as well as targeted students who may be slow learners, disabled, or disadvantaged either by income or language.

Differentiation as a teaching and learning strategy begins with agreement on the philosophical underpinnings and acceptance of a differentiated instructional environment as a primary teaching and learning platform. Once this underpinning is in place, practical questions will emerge. Since the teachers must know their students well enough to differentiate instruction for them, how does the teacher get to know students well and fast? How should they preassess (and later reassess) the skills of each student and determine the critical differences that must be addressed for each student over time? The students differ in interests, cultures, genders, learning styles, expression preferences, and even sexual orientation, to name a few. These are all in addition to academic strengths and weaknesses brought to the classroom from years of prior schooling experiences. While this vast list of differences seems daunting, some strategies can be effective in a variety of settings with diverse students to improve the odds of learning taking place frequently and at high levels.

This chapter includes strategies for leaders that can help address some of these and other pressing questions on what to do in classrooms to differentiate instruction.

Differentiating the Core Curriculum

Marzano (2003), in *What Works in Schools*, conducted a meta-analysis of 35 years of research on school effectiveness. He wrote that an essential or viable curriculum is one that is most appropriate for the student at particular benchmarks. It could be argued that schools have over the years reasonably provided essential curricula which if seriously undertaken by the student would indeed have them college- or career-ready upon graduation from high school. Therefore, the questions that cannot be skirted are: *Why are so many students not college- or career-ready? If the curriculum is not the problem, is access the issue?* Marzano (2003) defines an assured curriculum as an essential curriculum to which all students have access. This presents a conundrum. The CCSS are designed to provide rigor and a set of common standards crafted to produce college and career readiness, but this alone is no guarantee for success. Consider the students with special needs or those who have traditionally chosen to self-select out of high-level courses of study or those who were placed into pathways not leading to college or career readiness by school personnel? Differentiation can provide this access. According to the National Assessment of Educational Progress, students can comprehend but higher order thinking on an abstract level, as CCSS requires, will be a challenge. All students will need to link subject matter to synthesize, analyze, and integrate new ideas (Giouroukakis & Connolly, 2013).

Changes in Instruction

Leaders will need to propose and suggest ideas to differentiate the curriculum integrating higher order thinking skills. Changing the way teachers think about instruction is paramount (Bellanca, Fogarty, & Pete, 2012; Bellanca, Fogarty, Pete, & Stinson, 2013). Questions that leaders can pose include the following (Dana, Burns, & Wolkenhauer, 2013):

- How can I help teachers understand the complexities of the CCSS and proper implementation?
- How can we plan thematic units and integrate differentiated instruction and the CCSS standards for each department?
- How can we assure that multi-tiered systems, UDL, and technology are integrated to help students with disabilities?
- How will providing vertical planning time (the planning of education delivered in schools discussed between teachers of different classes or grades) and collaboration among teams help teachers?

By grade level or department, leaders will need to:

- perform formative and summative measures;
- study the data provided;
- review the subskills and performance tasks in CCSS;
- select and remediate thinking skills that seem problematic to students;
- determine the thread through the specific disciplines the skills are to be taught; and
- develop lessons that target cognitive skills.

Since thinking skills permeate the Common Core, teachers will need to find high-frequency thinking skills (i.e., clarifying, reasoning), then apply these skills succinctly and repeatedly until the students become independent in their levels of using the skill. Notable strategies include *explicit instruction* and *inquiry-based learning* as key concepts are infused into learning to increase differentiated, high-quality instruction.

Explicit Instruction

Explicit instruction is a form of direct instruction that engages the learner and has been shown to promote high achievement for general and special education students alike and can be implemented in any grade level or content area. This strategy is useful in conjunction with the CCSS because students are active participants in instruction. It can be used in diverse contexts and integrated into curricular areas. This technique adapts well in to CCSS because it integrates smaller units of learning into meaningful wholes. The students are cognitively engaged and the teacher frequently monitors the level of understanding from students. Generally, students are allowed to apply real-world skills in a meaningful manner. Important components include (Goeke, 2008; Archer & Hughes, 2010):

- Setting the stage (I will teach you how to interpret mathematical word problems): The teacher clarifies the purpose, objectives, goals, and standards. The lesson is connected to student's interest, background knowledge, and is linked to CCSS and previous learning.
- Explaining the lesson (I will tell you what to do): The task is divided into steps and differentiated for students. An explanation is provided as to why the lesson is important, how it is done, and how it is linked to real-world experiences.
- Modeling (I will show you what to do): The exact task is completed by the teacher using a "think aloud" methodology (talking while performing the task) and instructional connections are formed. Students are engaged and focused as they participate in the modeling process through the use of probing questions (using *Bloom's Taxonomy*).

- Guided practice (I will help you perform the task): The teacher uses graphic organizers to "capsule" the basic components of the lesson and provide cues to steps in the task. Steps are scaffolded and instruction is differentiated according to the needs of the student. Examples and non-examples are provided (Lenz & Deshler, 2004).

- Independent practice (I will allow you to perform the task alone): Students are to be kept on task while they practice the skills. The teacher must monitor to assure the student completes the task or if they need more guided practice.

- Assessment (I will assess your skill in performing the task): Assessments should assure that students have performed the task with at least 80% proficiency through formal and informal, formative and summative measures. The assessment should provide evidence that the student has mastered the concept or standard.

Instruction is scaffolded throughout the learning process, and differentiated instruction is freely integrated as each student is moving toward independence. Teachers should:

- encourage ideas;
- adjust to student understanding;
- diversify opportunities for student participation;
- assure that students actively participate (connect new concepts, skills, strategies);
- use graphic organizers;
- allow student response; and
- provide corrective feedback.

Inquiry-Based Learning

Inquiry-based learning is a real-world application that complements CCSS. It starts by posing questions, problems, or scenarios rather than presenting established facts. Inquiry strategies can provide teachers with a more clear view into the cognitive processes of the students as a lesson moves forward. At the beginning of a lesson, properly posed questions can serve as a formative measure assessing the knowledge and understanding of a given topic already possessed by the students. During a lesson, questions provide opportunities to see how much and how well the students are acquiring new information and skills. At the end of a lesson, questioning provides students with cognitive connections between yesterday's and today's learning and sets the stage for tomorrow's learning and whether reinforcing homework needs to be adjusted. A sample dialogue from a teacher to students at different stages of a lesson is presented in Table 9.1.

Table 9.1 Inquiry Examples

Beginning of lesson question

Teacher: Yesterday we talked about how the process of photosynthesis in green plants takes carbon dioxide from the atmosphere and produces oxygen. What might be the effects of global warming on this process?

Mid-lesson question

Teacher: We began the day with a question about yesterday's discussion of how green plants produce oxygen and how global warming might affect that process. Today we have been talking about non-green plants. I want you to think about when you have seen a non-green plant around your neighborhood. Where was it? Hypothesize how it survives without chlorophyll.

Lesson summary question

Teacher: Integrating science and social studies, can you think of how our discussion of plants might be connected to social studies where we are studying countries and the products they export?

Each of these questions was at the comprehension level or higher and connects disciplines. All questions were connected to previous and future learning with real-world examples. They are consistent with the Common Core's focus on higher level learning with real-world applications. The use of questioning as an instructional tool is not without challenges. In a research study on questioning in science classrooms at elementary, middle, and high school levels, Eshach, Dor-Ziderman, and Yefroimsky (2014) found that questions provoking higher level thinking are less frequently posed than those soliciting more low-level responses. They noticed that all teachers at all grade levels asked fewer _higher order questions_ compared with _middle order_ or _lower order questions_. Eleven out of the 17, in a typical class, are _lower order questions_. Consequently, leaders must be ready and able to assist teachers in changing the nature of classroom questioning, namely increasing the frequency of those that require higher level thinking responses.

The following key questioning strategies are based in part on the work of Cotton (2001) of the North West Regional Educational Laboratory and expanded by these chapter authors. They offer several tips for inquiry strategies that have proven to be effective in classrooms that can be used to further CCSS options:

- A teacher needs to be proficient at asking divergent, high-level questions.
- When planning questions for a lesson, it is a good idea to script questions at multiple levels of the cognitive domain (high, middle, and low).
- While it may be more difficult to ask grade-level questions at the higher levels of _Bloom's Taxonomy_ on measures, using them as regular classroom discussion questions is primary and a natural part of good teaching.
- For lower level questioning, the use of technological devices such as clickers or even student cell phone application can motivate students to engage while simultaneously providing the teacher with an overview of what students understand and which concepts need additional work.

- Questions asked at the higher levels of the cognitive domain typically indicate successful functioning at each of the lower levels of questioning.

- When asking a question, ask the entire class rather than pose the question to a particular child and then provide enough wait time for all students to consider possible answers before a specific student is chosen. Reinforce effort and use wait time. Let the student think through the answer. If the student cannot think of an answer, a proper teacher response might be, "Chuang, you really did some good thinking there, but the kind of animal I was looking for was 'primate.' Be ready, I will come back to you with another one, and I bet you will be ready for that one."

School Environmental Challenges and Solutions: Smoothing Rough Places

In order for educators, schoolwide, to successfully and fully differentiate the curriculum so that all students can succeed within the CCSS, there are some assumptions that are non-negotiable. Fundamentally, special and general education leaders must affirm the core value that capacity for learning can grow in a carefully designed environment (Dweck, 2006). The effective leader operationalizes the core value of differentiation for students and staff.

School-Based Leaders

Eilers and D'Amico (2012) discuss several essential elements in implementing the CCSS using differentiation. Since leaders are the main persons who are guiding teaching and learning in the institution, they have the responsibility for meeting the demands in this uncharted territory. They believe that the leaders will need to:

- *Establish a purpose.* Leaders must develop the mission and vision for the CCSS for their school—most importantly a way to guide instruction into a deeper coverage and integration of discipline areas of instruction. Analysis of the resources, workshops, materials collaboratively with the faculty is essential.

- *Align faculty and staff instructionally and philosophically.* Shifts in content and pedagogy are crucial. Present instruction must be realigned to include the scaffolding techniques associated with differentiated instruction. Total Instructional Alignment assures how and what we teach and assess are aligned (Carter, 2007). All teaching and learning is planned, taught, and assessed at grade level. A key to accomplishing the grade-level standard in planning, teaching, and assessment is a clear and unambiguous agreement across teachers in the school about what the student is to know and demonstrate in order to show mastery of concepts of a given standard. Some suggest that this agreement across teachers is best established through professional learning communities (PLCs; see Tables 9.1 and 9.2) (DuFour, 2004). If there is no clear agreement, there will be an inherent lack of focus within the teaching and learning system.

- *Organize intensive professional development for teachers designing instruction and assessments.* School-designed classroom instruction and assessments still provide the most reliable information for differentiation. Teachers will need ongoing professional development in CCSS teaching strategies and measures for each level.

- *Determine the stages of development.* Develop an agenda, a set of task that can be sequenced in stages, and set priorities for a practical preemptive structure and an action plan for each grade level.

- *Organize teachers into horizontal and vertical instructional teams.* Horizontal teams (by curricular objective, grade level, subject, etc.) provide consistency of instruction across different teachers teaching the same levels and concepts within the same standard(s). Common planning for PLCs is a typical practice to accomplish horizontal alignment. However, school leaders must be careful to observe that common planning does not lead to what we describe as *common teaching*. *Common teaching* is characterized by all teachers of a given grade level and subject (sixth grade math, for example) teaching the same concept on the same day and in the same way. Such *common teaching* is the antithesis of differentiated instruction. The work of vertical teams (all reading teachers in K–5 or all high school math teachers) when properly designed and implemented embodies the idea of internal customer service between colleagues up and down the grade ladder who depend on each other if their students are to steadily progress upward in their learning. Vertical teams assure that there are no gaps in curriculum, teaching, and learning so that when the sixth-grade student enters the seventh grade it is with the assurance for both the students and their teachers that they are ready for the next step (Lambert, 2002). Vertical alignment and vertical teams in place are an absolute requirement for guaranteed access to the curriculum—especially for targeted populations of students. Without the continuous process of educators focused on vertically aligning the curriculum, learning gaps for targeted populations will likely continue to grow ever wider making them even harder to close.

- *Genuine inclusion must start with the teachers, not the students.* If targeted students are to succeed in an assured curriculum, the teachers with specialized skills to help those youngsters must be fully functioning and consistent members of the horizontal and vertical teams. Neither the grade-level teacher, subject area teacher, nor the special teacher, alone, can likely meet the needs of targeted students such that they can achieve at their fullest potential. Therefore, school leaders and leaders for targeted students bear the responsibility of resolution, as a true team. Parity is important! The seed-change of this pertinent core value must be, "This is our classroom; how can we collectively and collaboratively do what we could not accomplish individually to insure the success of each student?"

- *Expectations from principals and superintendents must be communicated clearly and consistently that leadership and a commitment to differentiated teaching and learning are prerequisites.* This paradigm shift is essential to success and all are accountable to support and is equally important to accountability for this approach. Colleges of education should also infuse these principles into their teacher and leader preparation programs to ensure that future professionals entering the field understand that differentiated instruction is a norm to achieve the goals of the CCSS and not an ancillary remedial program.

- *Use PLCs to always stay focused on how to differentiate for the students who did not master the last summative assessments.* For those who did master it, use the PLC to design regrouping as preferred strategies (see Table 9.2).

- *Align instruction from standards to the classroom using the revised* Bloom's Taxonomy. *Standards are not specific learning objectives.* Not all learning objectives as produced by states or districts are clear, specific, and measureable. Make sure that every objective is clearly understood by every teacher who must teach it and every child who must demonstrate it.

- *Limit reliance on mass-market assessments.* Learn to create reliable classroom/ PLC formative and summative assessments. Work with local universities to conduct research validating the action research work within your site or school district as universities can be important partners for designing and testing the validity of assessments.

- *Provide specific feedback.* Provide continued support through corrective and specific feedback.

Special Education Leaders

The RTI and MTSS are key components for inclusion and the academic achievement of all students and have been included in systematic reform for quite some time. Special education and school leaders organize, prioritize, and manage these types of systems to assure the conditions for implementation are the core of differentiation for students at risk and students with disabilities. Staff will need sufficient time to accommodate changes in the current practices; therefore, leaders have the responsibility for the continual development of these types of models and must supervise and facilitate their proper use (Johnson, Smith, & Harris, 2009). Mellard and Johnson (2008) suggest that a PLC model (group of educators who share expertise and work collaboratively to improve teaching skills and the academic performance of students) be used to further these types of differentiation efforts. An example of a PLC is provided in Tables 9.2 and 9.3.

Table 9.2 Successful PLCs

Embrace the PLC philosophy

1 Every team member is responsible for the learning of every student on the team.
2 Every team member is responsible for the support and success of every other team member.
3 Be totally honest, but never judgmental.
4 Have an agreed-upon agenda shared prior to the meeting.
5 Focus 100% on problems of professional practice—2/3 on individual students; 1/3 on teacher/school issues.
6 Use a process to analyze problems and test solutions.
7 Conclude with a plan of what to accomplish prior to the next meeting.

Prepare for the PLC meeting

1 Review your students' performance on the last PLC team-developed common unit assessment.
2 Identify students who failed to master the formative and summative measures.
3 Gather examples of their work products to share.
4 Identify all students who failed to master the mini-lesson content.
5 Review the CCSS to be taught in (a) assessed areas and/or (b) reading, writing, and mathematics after the PLC meeting.
6 Identify any vague objectives.
7 Develop a meeting agenda based on items 1–6.

Focus on collegiality around problems of practice

1 Always have an agenda.
2 Appoint a time keeper.
3 Keep simple minutes with notes by agenda items.
4 Be honest about student and team performance.
5 Assume that every team member is doing the best they know how to do.
6 Take ownership and pride in student performance, not your design of learning activities.
7 Discuss the processes which need to be changed, improved, or invented so that all students can master the content. If an activity does not produce the results, do not fret; do not keep doing it, but do seek help and advice from your team!

Discuss student performance

1 Discuss performance on the objectives and assessments (formative and summative) since the last PLC meeting.
2 Discuss those students not performing at grade level overall.
3 Discuss those students who failed to reach mastery on (a) teacher-designed and (b) team-designed unit assessments and (c) mini-assessments.
4 The students do not have the prerequisite skills necessary to master objectives on assessments being discussed.
5 Are the students engaged with the work assigned?
6 Did the students have the prerequisite skills, but still failed to master the current content?
7 Create a plan to track the team's student performance over time.

(*Continued*)

Table 9.2 (Continued)

Discuss teacher/school issues

1 The key to discussing teacher-oriented issues during PLCs is to always keep them directly related to measurable student learning.
2 Many teacher-oriented issues will naturally flow from the discussion of students with prerequisite skills who still failed to master expected content.
3 Designing new activities to meet student learning needs is one of the joys of teaching, but is one of the riskiest things we do because we do not know at the outset if they will work.
4 Be sure that your design includes a method to determine if student learning was affected and that you set a date to discuss the results at a future PLC.
5 Use the Plan-Do-Study-Act Cycle to analyze problems, create solutions, and to check for results.

   Plan—When a problem occurs, plan how to address it.
   Do—Address the problem on a small basis before implementing organization-wide solutions. Study—Look at the results of the pilot implementation and make necessary adjustments or start over again.
   Act—Implement the plan on a large scale, then repeat the process in discussing problems and solutions.
6 If you are discussing a new learning activity that you have read about or seen, all group members are responsible for keeping the team on track by being ready to ask, "Is there data that it improved student learning?"
7 Discuss schoolwide factors negatively affecting student learning based on school effectiveness research (Marzano, 2003).

Measure each PLC meeting's success

1 Did we stay on the agenda?
2 Did we spend at least two-third of our time talking about individual student's performance?
3 Did we agree on a plan to reteach and reassess students who failed to master agreed-upon content from our last PLC meeting?
4 Do we collectively and individually understand and agree on EXACTLY what our students are to KNOW and DO between now and the time we meet again and have a process for building a common assessment?
5 Did we look at our PLC team student achievement on an ongoing basis?
6 Did we practice the Plan-Do-Study-Act?
7 Did we share assessed student work such as writing samples for feedback from our peers, and do we have a process to share and archive Things That Work (TTWs).

Table 9.3 Tracking PLC Team and Meeting Progress

Team: _____Date: _____

	1	2	3	4
Stay true to the PLC philosophy				
Every team member is responsible for the learning of every student on the team.				
Every team member is responsible for the support and success of every other team member.				
Be totally honest but never judgmental.				
Have an agreed-upon agenda shared prior to the meeting.				
Focus 100% on problems of professional practice—2/3 on students; 1/3 on teacher/school issues.				
Use a process to analyze problems and test solutions.				
Conclude with a plan of what to accomplish prior to the next meeting.				
Prepare for the PLC meeting				
Review your students' performance on the last PLC team-developed assessment.				
Identify students who failed to master the formative and summative assessments.				
Gather examples of their work products to share.				
Identify all students who failed to master the lesson content.				
Review the CCSS to be taught in (a) assessed areas and/or (b) reading, writing, and mathematics after the PLC meeting.				
Identify any vague objectives from the standards.				
Develop a meeting agenda based on items 1–6.				
Build PLC muscles: Focus on collegiality around problems of practice				
Always have an agenda.				
Appoint a time keeper.				
Keep simple minutes with notes by agenda items.				
Be honest about student and team performance.				
Assume that every team member is doing the best they know how to do.				
Take ownership and pride in student performance, not design of learning activities.				
Discuss the processes that need to be changed, improved, or invented so that all students can master the content.				

(Continued)

Table 9.3 (Continued)

Discuss student performance ...

...on the same set of objectives and assessment (formative and summative) since the last PLC meeting.

...of those students not performing at grade level (general teacher assessment).

...of those students who failed to reach mastery on assessments.

...of students who do not have the prerequisite skills necessary for mastery.

...of students not engaged with the work we assigned.

...of students with prerequisite skills, but still failed to master the current content.

... over time on PLC-designed common assessments.

Discuss teacher/school issues

Always keep them directly related to measurable student learning.

Looks at classroom activities which did not produce mastery learning.

Design new activities to meet student learning needs.

Design includes assessment and reporting components.

Practiced Plan-Do-Study-Act to analyze problems, create solutions, and to check for results.

Frequently asked of activities, "Is there data that it improved student learning?"

Discuss schoolwide factors, using school effectiveness research.

Measure each PLC meeting success

Did we stay on the agenda?

Did we spend at least two-third of our time discussing individual student's performance?

Did we agree on a plan to reteach and reassess students?

Do we agree on EXACTLY what our students are to KNOW and DO before we meet again and have an assessment plan?

Did we look at our PLC team student achievement on an ongoing basis?

Did we practice the Plan-Do-Study-Act process in discussing problems and solutions?

Did we share assessed student work for feedback from our peers and have a process to share and archive TTW?

Differentiation is the heart of any special education program. Special education leaders are aware of varied kinds of evidence-based practices such as research-based teaching routines and practical methods for lesson planning. Collaborating with school leaders, special educators are prepared to address academic diversity in schools. Special education leaders need to make sure that learning goals in relation to students' Individualized Education Programs (IEPs) are set as a priority (Ainsworth & Viegut, 2013). Samuels (2011) suggests that leaders use academic bookmarks tied to differentiation techniques. Special education and school leaders assist special and general education teachers to:

- *Align standards.* Standards-based IEPs should be aligned with the goals of differentiated individualized instruction. These goals should move the student toward grade-level CCSS targets.

- *Differentiation.* These techniques help students with disabilities function within the general education curriculum.

- *Functional skills.* Assure that the IEPs of students with severe disabilities are met as much as possible. Students should receive functional and academic skill instruction as needed within the CCSS framework.

- *Most feasible standards.* Choose standards that are going to profit the student and provide several avenues to show mastery.

- *Knowledge.* Have deep knowledge of the goals at each grade level and have a sound basis and a concrete plan to move to that academic goal.

Connections to Assessment

Formative assessments, frequent short tests, are a main tool for use in CCSS because measures like these are sensitive to differentiated instruction. These assessments are not used to determine grades but to define what students know and what needs to be differentiated. Passing or failing the grade is not the focus, rather instruction; the major onus is daily modified instruction according to the results of formative assessments. The purpose of teacher measures is to provide feedback so the learner can improve performance, thereby helping the students to take ownership of their learning (Black & Wiliam, 2009).

In the differentiated classroom, assessment is ongoing and daily and students are measured on their readiness for ideas and varied skills in the CCSS. These types of "dynamic assessments," when implemented, encourage student interaction and support and sustain and maintain learning that has occurred. Assessments like these motivate students as they are provided feedback that is sensitive to the learning that increases their success regarding particular skills or standards.

Formative assessments are about teaching and learning and represent reciprocal learning (Heritage, 2010). That is, the student, the teacher, and the leader gather important information. Both teacher and student can review the assessment and see strengths and weaknesses and assist students in understanding and making judgments about their learning (Heritage, 2010).

Leaders and teachers can collectively design formative assessments for every major theme in every grade level in the curriculum. Once infused and implemented into the school settings, these assessments demonstrate what learning has occurred and increases the probability of success because they are related to the lesson just presented. Formative assessments can easily be used in conjunction with scoring rubrics. Rubrics allow flexibility with grading and emphasize incremental learning.

There is a shift in using various assessment results (Bellanca et al., 2013). Shifts in instructional tools leads to shifts in instructional practices and measures. Leaders can assist this process by acting as a catalyst to provide tools that will help align CCSS and related to differentiated instruction and change the tradition of the assessment cycle from just test scores to analysis of student work. As more explicit assessment tools are designed, leaders can assure that the standards and assessment instruments have been truly aligned to the curriculum. Data analysis models can include (a) pre-assessments, (b) a plan for differentiation and reflection, and (c) then post-assessment.

Both teachers and leaders need to use multiple data sources and be aware of what kinds of data to collect. Both qualitative and quantitative data sources provide powerful student information. Data comes in so many forms such as journal reflections, electronic portfolios, lesson plans, rubrics, observations, checklist, and other artifacts. Leaders can provide staff development in relation to assessments that are used with the CCSS that should be included in measures of (Tomlinson & Allan 2000):

- models of differentiation, formative assessments, and rubrics;
- measurements of differentiation that can be used across units;
- effective use of other alternative assessments and differentiation;
- differentiation and scaffolding;
- evaluating degrees of differentiation that is needed by general and special education students alike; and
- differentiating by readiness, interest of lesson in sequence.

Applying Common Core Standards and Solutions

Leaders are reminded that while the CCSS set rigorous content expectations for all students and connect those expectations to particular grade levels, they do not prescribe the means by which mastery of the standards is to be achieved. This allows districts, and in some cases school-based leaders, to make their own decisions for planning and equipping teachers to establish appropriate benchmarks for mastering the Common Core curriculum. Tomlinson and Allan (2000) emphasize a results-based positioning. The teacher and the students must be assessed to determine level of change. Link CCSS, differentiation, and best practice to ensure that the learning needs of academically diverse learners are met. Leaders should assure that:

- The curriculum is connected to real-life experience to help students understand the connectedness of the disciplines being taught. Teachers and leaders collectively provide resources to assure that students' learning experiences relate to larger goals in the CCSS.

- Leaders, teachers, and students should understand and be able to explain the results of any learning experience in collective disciplines.

- Integrated disciplines should allow students numerous ways or the ability to have different products of learning to demonstrate.

- Students have input on designing task and products.

- Differentiated activities reflect high-level complex problems, ideas, issues, and skills that should propagate CCSS-type learnings.

- A number of formats that encourage differentiated formats such as small and large group discussion, Think-Pair-Share, open-ended problems should be included in instruction.

Research-Based Tips and Caveats

Leaders should:

- Encourage collaboration between special and general education teachers to develop in-depth CCSS activities that demonstrate the differentiation needs of learners.

- Encourage collaborative teams of general and special education teachers and specialists for planning lesson integration of disciplines.

- Allocate financial resources and encourage opportunities for professional development.

- Assess using formative and summative, formal and informal measures.

- Address differentiation in the context of higher cognitive curriculum.

- Align instruction with CCSS.

- Assure that the differentiated CCSS classroom has flexible grouping so that students will be responsible for their own learning and are allowed a variety of responses.

- Design and encourage shared vision and mission for CCSS.

(Continued)

(Continued)

- Measure both teachers and students to determine the level of skill instruction.
- Provide feedback to teachers with useful information to adapt instruction.
- Align assessments.
- Build a culture of collaboration.
- Guide professional development and strong collaboration teams.
- Ensure that teachers write learning targets that embrace cognitive rigor.
- Embed formative assessments within instruction as a teaching tool.
- Help teachers to identify common tasks and assignments.
- Develop PLCs that are key to learning for CCSS.

Summary

This chapter began with the story of Chuang. Clearly life has provided Chuang, a high school freshman, with more than his share of challenges: two years removed from his parents' deaths; living in a foster home with his brother; disinterested in school; seldom completes assignments; lagging in reading skills; and has changed schools four times since his parents passed away. However, Chuang does attend school, and he looks up to his brother who is doing well as a senior in the same school.

The typical question that quickly surfaces when the profession is confronted with targeted students with similar stories is this: Can the Common Core standards work for all students, even the Chuangs? If the profession answers "No," "Maybe," or "We will try," then their future is somewhat predictable, and the most profoundly negative notion in the lexicon of the education profession, "I taught it; they just did not learn it," is reinforced.

A similar but much more important question is this: Do schools control enough of the variables of learning to meet the expectations of the Common Core standards? To this question, some scholars such as Lezotte (2007), Marzano (2010), DuFour (2004), and Elmore (2000) answer, "Yes; we do." For them, the keys to this critical question are found in focus, control, and courage. We can focus on the components we can control (what happens at school), or we can focus on those things over which we have no direct control (what happens outside of school). Once we have established a focus on controlling those things under the control of the school that positively affect student learning for all students, we may find that this control begins to positively influence additional factors previously thought to be beyond the control of the schoolhouse, fueling optimism through motivated students, their parents or guardians, and ultimately community stakeholders. The very hard work of differentiation of instruction shows students and their families that school people care deeply, believe in and expect success, and show just how hard they are willing to work to bring their successful achievement to fruition.

Ultimately each educator must decide if Chuang is to be a temporary or permanent victim of life circumstances beyond his control as a minor child in our society. It takes courage to do the right thing, in the right way, at the right time for all children. Within the present structure of the American K–12 system, differentiating instruction to meet the CCSS offers hope for bridging achievement gaps and ensuring that all children meet them.

References

Ainsworth, L., & Viegut, D. (2013). *Common formative assessments: How to connect standards based assessments*. Thousand Oaks: CA: Corwin Press.

Anderson, L., Krathwohl, D., Airasian, P., Cruikshank, K., Mayer, R., Pintrich, P., . . . Wittrock, M. (Eds.). (2000). *A taxonomy for learning, teaching, and assessing: A revision of Bloom's taxonomy of educational objectives*. New York, NY: Pearson.

Archer, A. L., & Hughes, C. (2010). *Explicit instruction: Effective and efficient teaching (what works for special-needs learners)*. New York, NY: Guildford Press.

Bellanca, J. A., Fogarty, R. J., & Pete, B. M. (2012). *How to teach thinking skills within the Common Core: 7 key student proficiencies of the new national standards*. Bloomington, IN: Solution Tree Press.

Bellanca, J. A., Fogarty, R. J., Pete, B. M., & Stinson, R. L. (2013). *School leaders guide to Common Core*. Bloomington, IN: Solution Tree Press.

Black, P., & Wiliam, D. (2009). Developing the theory of formative assessment. In J. MacBeth & L. Moss (Eds.), *Education assessment evaluation and accountability* (Vol. 21, pp. 5–31). London, UK: Springer.

Carter, L. (2007). *Total instructional alignment: From standards to student success*. Bloomington, IN: Solution Tree.

Cotton, K. (2001). *Classroom questioning*. Retrieved from http://edc371-01.wikispaces.com/file/view/Classroom+Questioning.pdf

Dana, N. F., Burns, J. B., & Wolkenhauer, R. (2013). *Inquiring into the Common Core*. Thousand Oaks, CA: Sage.

Diamond, M., & Hopson, J. (1999). *Magic trees of the mind: How to nurture your child's intelligence, creativity, and healthy emotions from birth through adolescence*. New York, NY: Plume Publishing.

DuFour, R. (2004). What is a professional learning community? *Schools as Learning Communities, 61*(8), 6–11.

Dweck, C. S. (2006). *Mindset: The new psychology of success*. New York, NY: Random House.

Eilers, L. H., & D'Amico, M. (2012). Essential leadership elements in implementing Common Core State Standards. *Delta Kappa Gamma Bulletin, 78*(4), 46–50.

Elementary and Secondary Education Act of 1965, Pub. L. No. 89-10, 20 U.S.C. § 79 Stat. 27. (1965).

Elmore, R. F. (2000). *Building a new structure for school leadership* (pp. 1–46). Washington, DC: Albert Shanker Institute.

Eshach, H., Dor-Ziderman, Y., & Yefroimsky, Y. (2014). Question asking in the science classroom: Teacher attitudes and practices. *Journal of Science Education and Technology, 23*(1), 67–81.

Giouroukakis, V., & Connolly, M. (2013). *Getting to the core of literacy for history/social studies, science, and technical subjects, grades 6–12.* Thousand Oaks, CA: Corwin.

Goeke, J. (2008). *Explicit instruction: A framework for meaningful direct teaching.* Boston, MA: Pearson.

Heritage, M. (2010). *Formative assessment and next-generation assessment systems: Are we losing opportunity?* Washington, DC: Council of Chief State School Officers.

Johnson, E. S., Smith, L., & Harris, M. L. (2009). *How RTI works in secondary schools.* Thousand Oaks, CA: Corwin.

Lambert, L. (2002). A framework for shared leadership. *Educational Leadership, 59*(8), 37–40.

Lenz, B. K., & Deshler, D. D. (2004). *Teaching content to all.* Boston, MA: Pearson.

Lezotte, L. (2007). Introduction. In L. Carter (Ed.), *Total instructional alignment: From standards to student success.* Bloomington, IN: Solution Tree.

Marzano, R. J. (2003). *What works in schools: Translating research into action.* Alexandria, VA: Association for Supervision and Curriculum Development.

Marzano, R. J. (2010). Representing knowledge nonlinguistically. *Educational Leadership, 67*(8), 84–86.

Mellard, D. F., & Johnson, E. S. (2008). *RTI: A practitioner's guide to implementing response to intervention.* Thousand Oaks, CA: Corwin.

Samuels, C. A. (2011, January 12). Special educators look to align IEPs to common-core standards. *Education Week, 30,* 15.

Shore, R. A. (1997). *Creating a positive school climate.* Mt. Kisco, NY: The Plan for Social Excellence.

Shore, R. A. (2002). *Baby teacher: Nurturing neural networks from birth to age five.* Lanham, MD: Rowman & Littlefield.

Tomlinson, C. A. (1999). *The differentiated classroom: Responding to the needs of all learners.* Alexandria, VA: Association for Supervision and Curriculum Development.

Tomlinson, C. A. (2001). *How to differentiate instruction in mixed-ability classrooms* (2nd ed.). Alexandria, VA: Association for Supervision and Curriculum Development.

Tomlinson, C. A., & Allan, S. D. (2000). *Leadership for differentiating schools and classroom.* Alexandria, VA: Association for Supervision and Curriculum Development.